Amram Musungu has a compelling and unique story to share. He is a true, modern, Utah Pioneer."

Utah Governor Gary R. Herbert (2005-2021)

. . .

Amram was born bold in declaring the gospel. He is one of the chosen people the Lord placed on the surface of this earth. With Amram it's not just what he's saying—there's action. He recognizes goodness and wants to shout it out. If everyone was as missionary minded as Amram, the Church membership would double.

Freddie Thomas
Missionary who taught Amram in Kenya

. . .

Amram's story is inspirational in many ways, but what stands out to me is his example of unfailing faith. Despite how uncertain his future was, he remained determined to stay his course. Amram shows us in his journey that you can move forward making good decisions without having the outcomes laid out in front of you. By trusting in the Lord and being willing to accept His will, Amram is proof that the Lord will not only keep us safe but will use us to *accomplish great things. I am grateful to have been a part of Amram's life and will always consider him a great friend.*

Russell Price
Missionary who taught Amram in Kenya

. . .

I worked closely with Amram Musungu when I was serving as president of the Utah Salt Lake Mission. Amram was instrumental in organizing a Swahili-speaking branch. Together we worked with the stake president involved and organized the leadership of the branch, which included Amram as the branch president. He was a delight to work with, and I enjoyed our time together as he organized the branch and after. While I was there, the branch was a great success and attracted many Swahili-speaking members. Amram was a great leader and made everyone feel welcome and loved. He is amazing!

W. Blake Sonne
Utah Salt Lake Mission President

. . .

My fondest memories of Amram occurred while walking the dusty roads of Dar-es-Salaam, Tanzania, together as missionaries for The Church of Jesus Christ of Latter-day Saints. Amram and I served during a time when the Church in Tanzania was new, and the field was truly white and ready to harvest. Amram's rock-solid testimony of the restored gospel of Jesus Christ fueled his desire to share that testimony with everyone we came in contact with! He fully understood the urgency behind the work we were engaged in. The area we served in required a lot of walking, and Amram would always speed-walk to each appointment. One day I asked him if he could slow down a bit as he was literally leaving me in the dust! He responded by saying, "Come on, Elder, we have work to do!"

As I reflect on missionary days with Amram, I can't help but think of President Kimball's call for members of the Church to lengthen their stride. In my opinion, there is no better example of anyone who lengthens their stride better than Amram. He gave his heart and soul to the Lord's children in Tanzania, and he continues to serve the Lord with that same enthusiasm today. Whenever I think I am doing enough in my church service, I think of Amram and how he continues to leave me in the dust.

> Ben Gibson
> Missionary companion in Tanzania

. . .

My daughter met Amram some years earlier, so we always looked for him in any broadcast that included the Tabernacle Choir. I was thrilled when he entered the Master of Accounting program at Westminster College and became a student of mine. When he graduated, I made sure that he was recognized as our Outstanding Accounting Student at the commencement service. I am proud to call him a student of mine, but more proud to call him a dear friend.

> Ron Mano
> Professor at Westminster College

Amram Musungu with author Heidi Tucker

IV

To Elder [signature] Buchmiller

BRIDGE OF MIRACLES

THERE IS NO IMPOSSIBLE IN LIFE

love [signature] Heidi Tucker

HEIDI TUCKER

Published by Redstone Media 2022

ISBN 978-0-9966146-3-4

Order your copy at:

RedstoneMedia.org

dennis11yman@gmail.com

or

HeidiTucker.com

heiditucker@desertinet.com

DEDICATION

To all the sowers possessing

seeds of hope and faith

who find opportunities

to spread those seeds

throughout the world.

TABLE OF CONTENTS

KENYA

Figure 1

Mount Kilimanjaro as seen from Amboseli National Park.

CHAPTER ONE

▲▲▲▲

Do not pray for an easy life.

Pray for the strength to endure a difficult one.

Bruce Lee

▼▼▼▼

Amram's lungs burned as he pushed himself forward. His mother had taught him that rain was God's way of watering the crops on their two-acre farm, but Amram saw it as a soggy obstacle preventing him from getting to school on time. He tried to focus on positioning his bare feet around those slick patches of mud, but the rain dripping off the large banana leaf he held above his head was an impeding distraction.

Just keep running! I can't be late today.

Amram knew the punishment for tardiness too well. Cane beatings were the norm for such disregard of time or incomplete assignments, and students often hid in the banana plantations to hide their tears after the discipline. It was a lesson administered by schoolteachers and often felt for days.

School in Hamuyundi, Kenya, was comprised of a chalkboard nailed to a big shade tree on the outskirts of the village. Without official birth records, the single requirement for admittance to primary school was the ability to reach the right arm over the head and touch the left ear. It was a decent prediction of age. Not all parents in the village encouraged education, but Amram's parents understood it would create future opportunity and make their children's lives better. Born in 1978 as the sixth of nine children, Amram had seen an example set over the years by older brothers and sisters.

The crow of the rooster at four a.m. was nature's alarm clock. Amram had one pair of shorts and one shirt to last for a week's worth of school. Books were carried in a sack used to store rice, and transportation to school was a barefoot run through the African bush and shrub. What began as a seven-mile run in primary school advanced to a twenty-four-mile run in secondary school. An early-morning start was necessary to complete the distance and arrive on time. Amram worked hard to maintain his grades and attend school every single day, even when the weather didn't cooperate.

Suddenly, ten-year-old Amram yelped as he felt a searing pain in his foot. He fell to his knees and looked back at the foot that was now a mix of red blood and brown mud. He noticed the broken bottle in the path a short distance behind. The unseen shard of glass hidden in the mud had sliced the bottom of his foot.

Please continue. Don't ever give up.

Amram could hear his parents' encouragement in his mind. There were dozens of reasons not to finish school, and many children in the village dropped out, but Amram's parents were adamant about schooling for their nine children. Education would open doors to their future.

Get up! You must get up!

Amram wasn't sure if he was hearing his own or his parents' words in his mind. He believed their words of support and trusted that attendance and hard work would enlighten his future life. Above all, Amram wanted to make his parents proud.

Now the pain was throbbing, and it seemed to imitate the beat of Amram's heart, which was pounding in his chest. He peeked once more at the oozing wound and muffled a quiet sob. Amram figured he was about halfway to school and had to run another twelve miles. He would need to go just as far to run home. He let the rain rinse his foot for a moment while he considered the options. Perhaps the teacher would excuse his tardiness if he showed her the injury. Mother would bathe the foot in warm saltwater and clean the wound later that afternoon when he returned home from school.

Amram stood up and squared his small shoulders. He wiped the tears now mixed with raindrops and looked toward the mountains where the school was located. His brave, young heart knew what to do. Amram winced and took a courageous step.

. . .

"Come now! Gather around. We have some fruits and vegetables today from the garden and we must thank God for it."

Mother never missed an opportunity to pray for blessings and express gratitude for all the goodness in their lives. For as long as Amram could remember, Mother's prayers were a necessary and comforting part of their daily routine. Her words would lead this little family in unity and humble praise to God, but she knew in her heart they would also teach.

"God sees all of His children," Mother explained. "He loves each of us and we must pray always. Tell Him everything in our hearts."

Grateful words were said over the food. With nine children in the Musungu family, some nights there simply wasn't enough food to go around, but Mother reminded them to be grateful for the smallest portion. Some nights, Amram noticed that she went without. Other nights, the Musungu family dinner was a drink of water, a prayer, and a glimmer of hope for tomorrow.

Words of praise and love were said before bed. They felt blessed to have a home, knowing that many did not. The mud hut was small but clean. Mother swept the dirt floor every morning and afternoon, and they all slept together on the clean floor with the added comfort of dry banana leaves sewn together in two big sacks for a mattress and a single blanket for a cover. Any other children or cousins who needed shelter were welcomed and found a small place of comfort under the shared blanket.

Stories often came from the Bible. Mother and Father read God's words to the children every day, and a favorite framed scripture hung by the entry to the hut as a reminder.

Choose you this day whom ye will serve . . .

but as for me and my house, we will serve the Lord. (Joshua 24:15)

Father made sure music was an important part of expressing gratefulness to God in the household. Whether he was whistling a gospel tune on his own or gathering the neighborhood children in the living room for a couple of hours of singing, Father made the whole family fall in love with music. He knew that singing praises to God would keep children from running loose in the village and would soften their hearts in the process. Father's love for music made a big impact among many in the village, including the youth.

Father's influence continued at the Pentecostal Assembly of God village church where he directed a choir. Practices were held on a regular basis, and the only requirement was a commitment and the desire to make beautiful sounds. Father taught them to listen with their hearts and learn the beautiful harmonies by ear.

Amram loved his time in both the neighborhood and church choirs. In addition to singing, he also picked up a real talent playing the drums. Amram loved expressing gratefulness to God and watching his father's love and enthusiasm for music. It was contagious and made Amram want to sing from his soul.

I wander through the still of night,
When solitude is ev'rywhere--
Alone, beneath the starry light,
And yet I know that God is there.

I kneel upon the grass and pray;
An answer comes without a voice.
It takes my burden all away
And makes my aching heart rejoice.

· · ·

Sleep would not come.

The deep, patterned breathing of sleep was heard from some of his siblings, but Amram's thoughts had kept him awake most of the night. He shifted slightly on the banana leaves hoping the rustling wouldn't disturb his sleeping siblings. Amram could hear soft, muffled sobs coming from his mother across the room. His chest ached with an empty pain he had never felt before.

It was the first time Amram had seen his father weep. Earlier in the day, a tragedy hit the Musungu family when Amram's oldest sister was visiting on holiday with her two-year-old child. His sister had complained of not feeling well, then took a turn for the worse and died suddenly. There were no doctors. No explanations. Just the unthinkable.

So much potential in her life was unexpectedly gone, leaving her young child motherless. Amram's parents had sacrificed so much to help Amram's oldest sister attend schooling in the city, and the entire family saw her as an example of hope and promise. She was beautiful, intelligent, and loving.

Amram stared up in the darkness toward the roof of his hut. He tried to imagine the black sky lit only by stars and wondered if heaven was beautiful and light somewhere beyond those stars. When Amram squeezed his eyes shut to force his own vision of such a place, tears slowly rolled down his cheeks and dropped onto the bed of banana leaves that cradled his head.

Amram's parents had always taught him that the Lord sees all His children—even in remote corners of the world. Amram wondered if the Lord could see him now. There were so many questions burning in Amram's heart. *Why did she die? Why would God do this to me and my family? Will I ever see my sister again?*

They were ruminations that Amram would carry in his soul. Troubled thoughts that would travel with Amram on a future journey. Tender feelings that would one day be answered in a handshake.

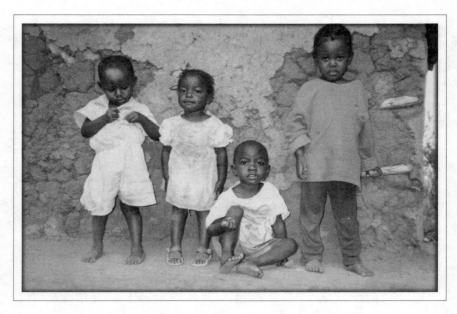

Amram (seated) – life growing up in the village.

Amram (shorter boy in 2nd row) attending primary school in the village.

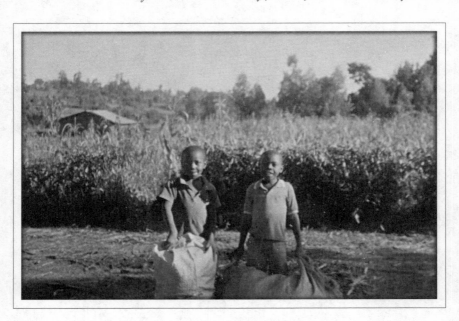

Amram (right) with cousin in village gathering grass for the cows.

CHAPTER TWO

The intensity of our desire to share the gospel is a great indicator

of the extent of our personal conversion.

Dallin H. Oaks

Elder Thomas lifted his eyes and scanned the valley below. It was an uncomfortable and heart-wrenching sight. He had never seen such poor living conditions in his life. Certainly, there must be something he could do to help these people.

It was a little corner of the world where Elder Thomas spent his mornings reading scriptures and pondering his part in serving God and the people of Kenya. The missionary apartment was located in a small, stone building on a hill, but on the rooftop were some stones of an unfinished wall where one could sit and look down into the valley. Elder Thomas left his home in Sierra Leone on the west coast of Africa as one of the first four missionaries to start the Church in Kenya, which was on the east side of Africa. The small Kibera Branch where he served was the first branch of the Church in Kenya.

The quiet place on the rooftop was a place Elder Thomas could ponder where he'd come from and how he could now make a difference in teaching others about Jesus Christ. His eyes left the scene before him and glanced down at the scripture that had tugged at his heart moments before:

O Jerusalem, Jerusalem . . . how often would I have gathered thy children together, even as a hen gathereth her chickens under her wings . . . (Matt 23:37).

His tear-filled eyes looked back at the panoramic view that stretched for miles. Kibera slum, located on the edge of Nairobi, was the largest slum in all of Africa and one of the largest slums in the world. The missionaries were prohibited from going into the area because it was dangerous. Elder Thomas felt a deep compassion for the people living in the area he could see and was saddened by his inability to help. After all, they were sons and daughters of a kind and loving Heavenly Father. He closed his scriptures and uttered a silent prayer.

Why should we not teach them?

· · ·

Amram took in his new surroundings. He had come to visit his older brother and to see the big city. The family had suffered emotionally and financially after the death of Amram's oldest sister, and his parents thought it would be best for Amram to visit with his brother and friends who lived in the Kibera slum in Nairobi. He was fourteen years of age, and perhaps there was a future opportunity to be found in the city of Nairobi. Amram knew he needed to eventually learn independence and was determined to remember his parents' teachings, move forward, and find good fortune.

The shanties in the slum were constructed of cardboard, wood, or any discarded piece of corrugated plastic that could be used as a wall or roof. Beds consisting of banana leaves or other padded materials were nudged into the corners of the square shanty with the exception of one corner, where a small kerosene stove was used to cook meals. A constructed table for food found its place in the middle. Dirt floors were swept, and people took pride in their own small space.

Although Kibera slum was located on the outskirts of Nairobi, there was no electricity, running water, or medical care. Ditches were dug through the passes in between shanties, and wastewater and sewage ran freely through the trenches. Most residents lived in extreme poverty, clinging to hope for a better future.

"Hello! Charles! It's Amram. I am here in Kibera visiting my brother."

Amram had found a public phone and called his cousin Charles to catch up on their lives. He hoped his cousin could find time to see him.

"Amram! Hey, tell me about the family. About everybody in the village."

Amram shared the details of his sister's death and all other happenings in the village. It had been a while since Charles had visited the Musungu home.

"You know — I'm glad you called," Charles said. "There are two missionaries that are teaching me this afternoon. They're teaching us new things about God and Jesus Christ. I think you should come and hear them. They're meeting at my house. We've been talking to them for a couple of months."

Charles's home was just a few miles outside the slum.

"Sure. Why not?" Amram replied. "I might grab Isaac and bring him with me. I'll see you soon."

Amram hung up the phone. He was excited to see Charles. He would convince his other cousin, Isaac, to come along. It would be a great opportunity to see each other.

Missionaries? Amram's curiosity was piqued.

. . .

"Hi."

Amram had knocked on the back door of Charles's house not a moment earlier. Suddenly it was opened with a jerk, and there stood a young man. Not just any young man—a white man.

"Glad you could come. Amram, is it?"

Amram nodded his head in response. He had never been spoken to by a white man. Charles hadn't said anything about this. The white man extended his hand to initiate a handshake.

"I'm Elder Price."

Elder Price left his home in Arizona to serve as one of the first white missionaries in the country of Kenya. The Kibera Branch was his first assignment, and he was eager to work hard. He had seen the slums from a distance, and he hoped that one day the Church might grow in Kenya. Elder Price was certain all the people throughout the country would really benefit and be blessed by the message he was there to deliver, but the odds were stacked against the people in the slums. How would they ever get out? Perhaps a message of hope—deep, eternal hope—and a knowledge that the Savior loved them would at least bring peace and maybe even inspire them to lift themselves out of some of their circumstances.

Amram met Elder Price's gaze and then reached out and grabbed his hand. It was the first time Amram had ever shaken a white man's hand. An unexpected feeling of familiarity and peace washed over Amram, and it caught his attention. As Elder Price motioned for the two of them to come inside, the two cousins walked inside to see another missionary extending his hand.

"Hi, Amram. I'm Elder Thomas."

These two men should have been strangers, but they felt like old friends. More than that—they felt like family. Amram felt surprisingly comfortable.

Why do I feel this way? It's like I know them . . . trust them.

Amram and Isaac took a seat next to Charles, eager to hear what the two missionaries had to say. Amram's eyes were wide in anticipation of their message, and he hoped that as they spoke their words it might explain why his heart was beating so fast. He sat up straight and focused on the two missionaries sitting across from him.

"Really? Eighty to ninety missionary discussions every week?"

The mission president in Kenya picked up the phone to call Elder Thomas and Elder Price after reading an email detailing their statistics for the work in the Kibera Branch.

"Yes, President. That's right. That's an accurate total of all lessons we've given in this area. There's this boy named Amram, and he's on fire. He's bringing family members, friends, anybody on the street who will listen. They all want to hear what Amram is so excited about in our missionary discussions," Elder Thomas explained.

In Amram's first lesson, he listened intently as the missionaries explained gospel truths carefully and slowly. Like so many in the country, Amram spoke both Swahili and English. He was less comfortable with English, which he had learned in school, and felt shy when expressing himself in the second language. The missionaries could see Amram's hesitancy in speaking and wondered if he was really understanding the lessons, which were in English.

Those concerns were quickly dismissed in the second appointment when Amram showed up with three more cousins, the reading assignment in his Book of Mormon completed, and a list of questions. Clearly the soft-spoken boy was bright and eager to learn more. Every week, Amram brought more people and soon the discussions had to be moved to a rental home in which they held church so there was room for everybody.

Where is the adversity?

As a new missionary, Elder Price had expected resistance to his message of the gospel. *This is too easy; are the people here for the right reason?* He hoped this humble group of investigators would have some staying power in the Church. They needed solid, righteous leaders in this area of Africa.

The missionaries stood at the front of the room, anxious to deliver their prepared remarks. They looked over the crowd of faces longing for their message. Amram sat among the crowd, smiling with satisfaction at the attendance. Elder Thomas glanced over at Elder Price as they both realized what was happening. They weren't allowed to teach within the slum boundaries, but Amram was bringing people from the slum to *them*. The desire of both missionaries' hearts was taking place through the work and zeal of a fourteen-year-old boy named Amram.

The lessons continued over the weeks. Amram set the ultimate example, always showing up on time with assignments completed. He was becoming more comfortable in expressing himself and asking questions in English. The missionaries often called on Amram to explain in his own words what they were teaching.

Many accepted the invitation to walk several miles with Amram and attend church on Sunday. Bare, dusty, or muddy feet were rinsed with water from a spigot outside the structure out of respect for God and their little house of worship. They wore the cleanest clothing they had and flip-flops on their feet.

The missionaries prayed these new investigators would feel the Spirit during the church meetings. They raised their voices in harmonious song with other members of the congregation to praise God for their lives and blessings. Hymns took on a new meaning as these Kenyans felt and expressed their testimonies in joyful devotion and gratitude.

We love thy house, O God,
Wherein thine honor dwells.
The joy of thine abode
All earthly joy excels.
It is the house of prayer,
Wherein thy servants meet,
And thou, O Lord, art there,
Thy chosen flock to greet.
We love the word of life,
The word that tells of peace,
Of comfort in the strife,
Of joys that never cease.

. . .

"You mean I will see my sister again?"

The question came from Amram's soul as they were studying the afterlife and the temple. The missionaries helped those in attendance understand what it meant to be an eternal family and how that fit into the plan of salvation.

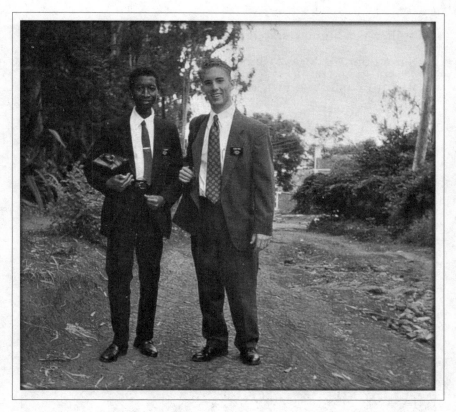

Elder Thomas and Elder Price who baptized Amram.

Amram stared at Elder Thomas for confirmation. It was all coming together—previous lessons, answered questions, and his study of scripture. God's plan really *did* have a purpose and made perfect sense. Amram knew it would make him a better person if he applied the principles to his own life. He believed it could help so many people, but he *felt* the personal application to his own family.

He sat quietly for a moment as his mind and heart connected.

"I believe this is true, and I want to be baptized," Amram declared.

It was a humble statement that would change Amram's life forever. A door to a new path had been opened. What no one knew was its future impact on the world.

KENYA

Figure 2
Elephants grazing in the Maasai Mara National Reserve.

CHAPTER THREE

We can all be more consistently involved in missionary work

by replacing our fear with real faith.

M. Russell Ballard

Amram placed his hands firmly on the wooden ladder and looked up the side of the water tank. It would require several steps to climb to the top of the outside of the tank, which also served as a baptismal font in the backyard of the rental home that the local congregation used as a meetinghouse. There were large trees and tall, lush grass in the area surrounding the tank, and it created a beautiful setting for the sacred ordinance on the seventh of June, 1992.

Amram paused for a moment and looked down at the white baptismal clothing the missionaries had given him to wear. He felt a sense of peace. He was doing this for God—no matter what the consequence. Amram whispered a silent prayer. *I am willing, dear Heavenly Father. I want to be baptized just like Jesus. But will I die today?*

Amram's mind wandered back to sermons in the Pentecostal Church. The Pentecostals taught that baptism by immersion in another church meant certain death. If that was true, Amram guessed that his heart would stop as soon as the water washed up over his head. Although he had been assured by the missionaries that death was not a consequence of baptism, a sliver of fear from earlier teachings remained in Amram's mind.

Weeks ago, Amram had made his own baptismal commitment in a quiet prayer. He didn't talk about this important decision to his family or friends because he didn't want any opposition. Amram understood that eventually he could attend the temple and be baptized for his sister. It was that thought along with the burning desire to be a part of this church that brought him to this humble, holy place. If necessary, Amram was ready to sacrifice his life for this gospel. His fingers tightened on the wooden ladder.

Amram took his first courageous step up the ladder and then loosened his grip to reach upward and pull himself toward the top. When he arrived at the top, Elder Thomas stood smiling in the water tank. Amram scaled over the top and into the tank. Elder Thomas took him by the hand and bowed his head in prayer, then performed the baptism.

Amram shot up out of the water and reached for his chest. He could feel his heart pounding.

I am alive!

He looked over at Elder Thomas, and the two embraced. A comforting wave of peace and love surrounded them; each felt the Spirit and recognized the importance of the moment. It was a quiet, sacred moment that would launch a whole new journey for Amram. This was just the beginning.

Amram took a deep breath as he saw the meetinghouse down the street. This would be the first time he would attend church as a member. Amram was among the first few hundred to be baptized in the Kenya Nairobi Mission, which had been created only months earlier in July 1991.

After the seven-mile walk from the shanty in the Kibera slum, Amram rinsed his feet and was ready to embrace this new life and religion. He entered the front door and found a seat in the back of the chapel. There were a few missionaries and other members of the congregation talking in hushed tones and a few people sitting in the front of the room. Amram assumed they would be speaking and hoped he wouldn't be required to do such a brave thing. As much as he had used his basic English with Elder Thomas and Elder Price, Amram was still reluctant when it came to his second language. Speaking English in front of a group was certainly out of his comfort zone.

Amram's eyes were scanning the room to watch those who were arriving when the branch president noticed him and began walking toward him. The branch president, who was from America, recognized Amram from the baptism and had heard from the missionaries about this energetic boy.

"Hello, Amram. It's great to see you!"

Amram smiled a little and shifted nervously in his seat.

"Would you be willing to give the opening prayer today?" the president asked.

"No," Amram uttered. He couldn't believe he was being asked.

"I'm sure you can do it, Amram. We want to hear from you." The branch president stood silently, waiting for a different answer.

Amram hoped he would walk away and ask someone else— someone who was older and smarter. But the president wasn't backing down.

I guess I need to do this. Maybe if they all close their eyes for the prayer, they won't see me.

"Okay, I can do it," Amram answered in a voice barely louder than a whisper.

The branch president patted Amram on the shoulder. He knew this boy was full of potential, even if the boy himself didn't see it yet.

. . .

Sweet is the work, my God, my King,
To praise thy name, give thanks and sing,
To show thy love by morning light,
And talk of all thy truths at night.
Sweet is the day of sacred rest.
No mortal care shall seize my breast.
Oh, may my heart in tune be found,
Like David's harp of solemn sound!
My heart shall triumph in my Lord
And bless his works and bless his word.

Thy works of grace, how bright they shine!
How deep thy counsels, how divine!

After the service, the branch president again approached Amram.

"Hey, Amram I would like to talk to you for a minute."

"Sure. Okay, great."

The branch president looked at the fourteen-year-old boy standing in front of him. This boy was still referring people to the missionaries, and the work was exploding. The president had never seen such a spirit of missionary work in someone so young—both young in the gospel and young in age.

"I'd like to give you a calling, Amram," the president said.

"Okay. What's a calling?"

"It's a responsibility here in our branch. Working with people. Calling and visiting. My heart tells me you're the one for this important calling," the president continued.

Amram's face lit up. He would love any responsibility here. Amram knew this church was like a new home to him. The feeling he had here was one of assurance and confidence that he had made a very good decision and was in the right place.

"I'd like to call you to be a branch mission leader."

"What is that?" Amram asked. *As a brand-new member of the Church, I still have so many things to learn.*

"Well, you'll be meeting with the missionaries every week and helping them find and teach people who are interested in learning about the gospel. They'll help you understand the responsibilities.

I have a lot of confidence in you, Amram."

Amram knew this was going to be hard for him, but he had done hard things before. Everything in his life had been hard, but his parents had taught him that good things come from hard work.

"Sure," Amram said with a shy smile.

. . .

"I have something for you, Amram," Elder Dewall said.

Elder Dewall and his wife were from Utah, and they were now serving a fulltime mission together. A large, strong man, Elder Dewall had been in the United States Navy for most of his life. He had noticed Amram and taken a special interest in the boy.

"I want to give you one of my white shirts. You're a missionary now, Amram, and this is yours. Your very first white shirt."

Amram's eyes widened. The shirt was huge, but he would tuck it into his shorts and make it work. *I'll look like a real missionary now.*

"Oh, and here's a tie. It's a clip-on tie—easy on and easy off."

Amram didn't have adequate words to express the amount of gratitude he felt in his heart for this man. He would soon be meeting with the Dewalls every week as they drove around meeting with a number of families. Amram watched and learned as this couple missionary loved and reached out to families throughout the area. He quickly became more and more comfortable bearing his own testimony and telling his conversion story. That same willingness was now extending to many members of his own family, and several of his cousins were introduced to the missionary lessons.

Amram never missed an appointment, and he attended all the missionary meetings. He eventually overcame his shyness about speaking in church as he was required to stand at the pulpit each week and report on families who were being taught. Amram also worked directly with the branch members trying to motivate them to refer their friends and family members to the missionaries. The training he received by all the missionaries was priceless, and they in turn depended on him to occasionally use his Swahili language skills when needed in missionary discussions.

Amram's decision to stay with his brother in Kibera wasn't difficult. Working every day with the missionaries gave purpose to Amram's life and helped him develop new leadership skills as he organized and assisted in teaching the investigators. He was happy serving the people and serving with the missionaries in the area, so his parents supported his decision to stay with his brother and cousin. They were proud of his new independence and could hear the joy in his voice.

On a recent visit to Kibera, Amram's father had given his son an unexpected gift. In fifteen years, Amram had never owned a pair of shoes, but his father wanted to pay for Amram's first pair. In the streets of Nairobi, a shoemaker measured Amram's foot for black leather wrapped around his foot and a piece of tile secured to the bottom. Although the shoes were a bit heavy and cumbersome in the mud, Amram appreciated the thoughtful gift. It made him feel good to be seen wearing shoes.

Some leaders from the Pentecostal Church in the Kibera area learned about Amram, the story of his baptism, and his eagerness to share his testimony of the Church with others. They came to his brother's shanty to discourage his passion and to call him names like *Mormon* or by names of other prophets in the Book of Mormon, like *Moroni* or *Nephi*. Amram just put his head down and went to work. He always forgave those who mistreated him, endured the persecution, and was never offended by the name-calling; after all, these great prophets accomplished so much, and he was honored to be called by the names of worthy men of God. Amram held tight to his testimony, believing with his whole heart and soul and recognizing the joy it brought to his life.

They don't know what I know.

. . .

"There goes the future of the Church," said Elder Richard P. Lindsay, a member of the Second Quorum of the Seventy and the Africa Area Authority who saw Amram working with the missionaries at the first district conference in Kenya. "There are blessings that will come to the Church in Africa because of members like Amram, who put the gospel of Jesus Christ first in their lives."

The mission president nodded in agreement with Elder Lindsay. Everybody who was involved with the Church in Kenya knew Amram's name. It was at this district conference that Amram received the Melchizedek Priesthood in his teenage years. In the two years since his baptism, Amram had learned to study and pray and give the missionary discussions in both English and Swahili. His influence reached far and wide; hundreds had either been referred or taught by Amram.

The group of missionaries opened and closed the conference by singing inspiring words of testimony. Elder Lindsay smiled at the eager group and felt the spiritual light emanating from them. He knew this was just the beginning for Kenya. Elder Lindsay noticed Amram sitting on the end of a wooden bench, singing the words of the hymn. Amram nodded as if agreeing with the lyrics and committing with his whole heart.

I have work enough to do,
Ere the sun goes down,
For myself and kindred too,
Ere the sun goes down:
Ev'ry idle whisper stilling
With a purpose firm and willing,
All my daily tasks fulfilling,
Ere the sun goes down.

. . . .

Amram clutched his fingers tightly around the paperwork in his hand. "Hello, my name is Amram Musungu. Is President Brown available? I have something for him." This was an important moment for Amram, and he hoped the mission president would have a moment to visit with him.

"Hello, Amram, I continue to hear great things about you," President Brown said with a grin. He had recognized Amram's voice from his office and stepped out to greet him. "Everybody in this area knows your name, and that says a lot. What brings you to the mission home today?"

"I have completed the missionary application you gave me." Amram thrust the paperwork toward President Brown. "I'm not nineteen yet, but I want to be ready when I am called."

"Come, have a seat," President Brown said, motioning to a chair in his office. "Let me take a look at your papers. You and I have talked before about your desire to serve a full-time mission in the future."

"Yes," Amram confirmed. It was the greatest desire of his heart.

"Well, I believe the Lord needs you sooner than expected," President Brown said.

"Really?" Amram exclaimed. "Missionary work is my life. There is no greater joy. How can I help?"

"Elder Musungu. . . ."

President Brown paused with emphasis on the new title. This was unprecedented, because Amram was only seventeen years of age, but he felt certain of the request. He would mail the paperwork to Salt Lake City immediately; there was no time to waste.

"Elder Musungu, I'm calling you to serve a two-year mission

in the Kenya Nairobi Mission."

Amram wondered if President Brown could hear his pounding heart. It beat with such force that he was sure it was audible to more than his own ears. Amram believed he should always sustain his church leaders. His mind raced with excitement.

I am willing to do this. I want to do this.

"And Elder Musungu," President Brown continued, "I need you to report to the mission home tomorrow morning."

Amram (4th from right) baptism by Elder Thomas and Elder Price on June 7, 1992.

KENYA

Figure 3
Zebra roaming the dusty landscape.

CHAPTER FOUR

▲ ▲ ▲

God does not begin by asking us about our ability,

but only about our availability,

and if we then prove our dependability,

he will increase our capability.

Neal A. Maxwell

▼ ▼ ▼

Amram knelt by his bed in the humble shanty he had called home within the rows of the Kibera slum. It would be the last time he slept here for two years. He wasn't sure where he would rest his head tomorrow night after his first official day in the mission field. Tears of gratitude fell down his cheeks as he thanked God for the opportunity.

Amram had wanted to be a full-time missionary for the Church since his baptism—something that was no secret to God or anyone else who knew him. Since the day he was baptized, Amram declared his desire to anyone who would listen. He always added, "I'll be able to go as soon as I turn nineteen," Amram proudly exclaimed, "and I want to be ready."

But this? What an unexpected blessing! Amram thanked God

for hearing the whisperings of his heart. What a tender mercy to be asked to serve so soon. The special permission granted for the early calling felt like a miracle from God. Earlier that evening, Amram had quickly written a letter to his parents telling them of the unexpected plan. Hamuyundi was eight hours away, so the news would have to be delivered in writing and not told in person. He knew they would miss him but be proud of his decision to be—in their own words—a preacher. Those who gave service to God were always honored.

Amram finished his prayers and rolled onto his bed. His young mind raced with anticipation. President Brown had said missionaries would pick him up tomorrow and take him to a clothing store in Nairobi to purchase a suit, white shirts, and all the missionary attire. The Church would provide the financial support.

His thoughts focused on the little branch he would be leaving. What a blessing the Kibera Branch had been in his young life. He had worked so hard to bring people there and wondered who would take over his responsibilities. Amram loved those with whom he had worked and served for years.

What about the sacrament preparation on Sunday? My friends won't know where I am.

Then Amram slowly smiled. His eyes glistened as he thought of his oldest sister.

I bet she's proud of me.

Amram's testimony ensured that he would see her again as part of his eternal family. That understanding of the plan of happiness was part of what inspired him to be baptized. Now he would take that knowledge and share it with other families throughout Kenya. It was a message of love, peace, and hope.

. . .

There weren't enough hours in the day. Between the paperwork, phone calls, and keeping everything organized in the mission, it was more than a full-time job. Elder Thomas had fulfilled his two years as a missionary but asked to extend that calling for two additional months. He was the assistant to the mission president and worked hard in the office to support President Brown and ensure the Kenya Nairobi Mission was running as efficiently and smoothly as possible. Elder Thomas was determined to finish on a high note.

"Elder Thomas, I've made a decision that will impact you," President Brown announced. He sat in the chair across the desk from Elder Thomas and smiled. "I want to call a companion to work with you. He won't be an assistant to me, just a companion to you, and I want you to train him and teach him everything you know. I feel like you're probably going to know this guy."

President Brown's smile widened. Elder Thomas sat up straight in anticipation.

"I'd like you to be the first trainer for Elder Musungu."

Elder Thomas bowed his head as waves of emotion filled his senses. It was a full-circle moment. He wanted to finish his mission on a high note, but never could have anticipated he would serve as a companion to someone he had baptized two years earlier. And not just anybody. Amram.

. . .

"Okay, Elder Musungu, watch me. It isn't hard—it just takes some practice."

Amram watched as Elder Thomas created the loop, pulling the tie in then out to make the knot. Nobody had ever taught Amram how to tie a tie because he had never owned a real one before. What a great blessing to be working side by side with Elder Thomas. Amram thanked God every day for the honor.

"If we're going to go out tracting, you need to look like a missionary with a real tie—not those clip-on imitations," Elder Thomas quipped.

Elder Thomas had approached President Brown after a month of training with Amram in the mission office to propose the option of assigning them a nearby area to proselyte. Elder Thomas had heard rumors of Amram's enthusiastic support of the missionary program back in the Kibera Branch over the last two years, but before Elder Thomas finished his mission, he wanted to ensure that Elder Musungu could knock on doors and teach the discussions on his own. Amram was now standing in front of the mirror adjusting the knot in his tie.

"All right, Elder Musungu, you look more than ready. Let's do this."

Elder Thomas shook his head and just watched the process unfold. Never before had he trained someone who served right from the start with vigor and conviction as Elder Musungu did. It was clear that he was in his element—comfortable approaching everyone and yearning to share his testimony with anyone who would listen. Amram had not only prepared himself for the past two years by learning the discussions and memorizing scriptures, but he had a love for the people and a real hunger for missionary work that was beyond his age.

Occasionally, they found themselves talking to a family who struggled with the English language. Elder Thomas trusted this new missionary companion had the capacity and spirit to teach and testify in Swahili if needed. Elder Thomas knew just enough Swahili to get around the streets, but to sit back and watch Elder Musungu teach with passion and fervor in his native language of Swahili was enlightening and inspiring. For an English-speaking mission, this was an unexpected blessing of serving with Elder Musungu.

Amram's face fell as he talked on the phone with someone at the mission office. Elder Thomas noticed the concerned features and bleak countenance. Amram hung up the phone and turned to face Elder Thomas.

"They just got word from my family that my dad is seriously ill with malaria," Amram said. His hand rubbed his forehead then slid back across the top of his head. "I don't know what to do."

"You know what?" Elder Thomas replied. "Let's fast and pray for his recovery. You and I together."

"You will fast with me?"

"Of course," Elder Thomas replied. "Let's begin right now. The Lord will do His work so you can continue to do yours."

. . .

Amram quickly hung up the phone at the missionary apartment and twisted around to face Elder Thomas.

"My dad—he's coming here right now! I can't believe it."

Amram's father had quickly recovered from his illness and, having received the address of the missionary apartment from one of Amram's friends in Kibera, wanted to surprise his son with an unexpected visit. He knew Amram had worried and prayed for him and wanted to show God's answer to those prayers in person. They had never really been able to say goodbye when Amram received his mission call, and Amram's father knew he wouldn't see him for another two years.

When Amram heard the knock at the apartment door, he quickly threw open the door to see his father standing there with a huge smile on his face. Amram ushered his father inside and the two began to catch up on their lives, including the miraculous recovery from malaria.

"Look at you!" Amram's father smiled. "You look like a real preacher!"

Amram's father had taught his children to love God and to show that love by serving others. Now his son was doing that in his own way. He loved Amram and could see a glimpse of the man he was becoming. He looked at his son and spoke from the heart.

"I just want to tell you to stay close to God. If you follow His teachings, your life will be a blessing to many people."

Amram and his father stood together as Elder Thomas took a picture with his camera. It would be nice to have the memory preserved, but film couldn't possibly capture the warm, tender feeling that filled the room.

As they prepared to part, Amram shook his father's hand. "It's so good to see you, Dad."

"I'm proud of you, Son."

Amram watched as his father walked down the road toward the corner. How he loved this God-fearing man who was so humble and kind. What a tender blessing to feel his presence once more.

Amram's eyes continued to watch his father until he turned the corner and was out of sight. His heart burned with gratitude and tears filled his eyes as he stared off into the distance. So many emotions swirled within Amram's chest.

"Elder Thomas, thank you for helping me to trust. For teaching me that miracles can happen from prayers." Amram's eyes continued to focus on the empty street before him, clinging to the vision of his dad, who was now full of light and health. "Life without prayer is like eating food without salt—without all the flavors you need and desire. We just need to have faith, right? I want to teach everyone to trust and have faith in their prayers. I have seen for myself that prayers are answered."

Amram turned to face the person who had baptized him just more than two years earlier. It was only a matter of days before Elder Thomas would be returning home.

"Everything that is happening to me is because you taught me. You're still teaching me. My baptism is the greatest thing to ever happen to me." Amram shook his head in wonder as he marveled the many blessings in his life. "Thank you for that," Amram said softly.

"Elder Musungu, it's not me," Elder Thomas insisted. "I was just a young man called by the Lord to serve a mission. It's because of *your* faith and commitment—*your* action—that your life has changed."

It had been an honor for Elder Thomas to serve the last two months of his mission with one of his first converts. Truly it was the highlight of his two-year mission and a recognized tender mercy from the Lord.

"It's you, Elder Musungu. *You* changed your life."

Amram as a missionary.

Photo taken in Amram's missionary apartment.
Elder Musungu, father, Elder Thomas.

KENYA

Figure 4
Crowded streets in Nairobi.

CHAPTER FIVE

▲▲▲

Everybody can be great . . . because anybody can serve.

You don't have to have a college degree to serve.

You don't have to make your subject and verb agree to serve.

You only need a heart full of grace.

A soul generated by love.

Martin Luther King Jr.

▼▼▼

"Tanzania?" Elder Price repeated.

"Yes," President Brown confirmed. "You are one of a few missionaries that we are transferring over to Tanzania. It's time to open up that area, and I'd like you to finish your mission there."

"I'll go wherever I'm needed, President," Elder Price stated. This was a surprise. He had expected to serve his whole mission in Kenya before returning home to Arizona.

"You'll start with a couple weeks of language training in Swahili," President Brown continued. "A large majority of the people over there will speak that language."

Elder Price was grateful that a couple of Kenyan missionaries were included in the group being transferred. Their Swahili language skills would be critical in both teaching and keeping everybody out of trouble. His mind raced back to Amram. There had been rumors floating throughout the mission that Amram had served as a branch mission leader in the Kibera Branch and that he was now serving a full-time mission in Kenya. His reputation and missionary zeal were known to many, but Elder Price had witnessed it firsthand. Elder Price smiled as he thought about the unstoppable teenager who had been a bright light in the first months of his mission and whose example had defined the term *member missionary*. Elder Price would never forget those early experiences with Amram.

Wouldn't that be amazing if our lives came together again in Tanzania?

. . .

They were at a standstill. The language barrier had become an issue, and although this family seemed eager to hear what these missionaries had to offer, they were struggling to fully comprehend the message in English.

Elder Price looked over at Elder Musungu. Elder Price smiled and nodded his head. It was time to hand the reigns over. Swahili words of testimony began to fill the room as Elder Musungu opened his heart to share a gospel message. It was a sight to behold.

This was the highlight of Elder Price's mission, and it started with a phone call from President Brown letting him know that Elder Musungu was on his way to Tanzania and was assigned to be his final companion. He had hoped that maybe their paths would cross at zone meetings, but to serve with him was an unimaginable and unexpected blessing.

There could be nothing more rewarding than witnessing and serving with this young man who had introduced himself as Amram with a handshake two years ago. To sit beside Elder Musungu and hear him explain to investigators how he started his journey in the gospel and gained his testimony was so rewarding. Although Elder Musungu was relatively new in the Church, he expressed his views so freely and testified how it changed his life.

It was an answer to Elder Price's prayer that began two years ago. There had been doubts about the effectiveness of teaching those who struggled with such poverty in the slums. He had wondered if they were doing the right thing by committing people to baptism who could barely make ends meet. It was so difficult for many to even get to church on Sunday. Yet, here was the answer right in front of him.

It was a testament to Elder Price that the Lord knew his heart and had answered his burning question.

. . .

"Elder Musungu, we can't go in there. That's the Prime Minister's house."

"Of course, we can go in there. God is no respecter of persons. We need to go and knock on all these doors," Elder Musungu replied.

Amram's new companion wasn't so sure. This was an area where many military leaders, politicians, and members of parliament lived. Often there were barking dogs or a strong security presence that was intimidating to most but that certainly did not deter Elder Musungu.

Sometimes doors were opened with an invitation to step inside, and sometimes conversations were conducted with security personnel, but wherever Elder Musungu tracted, he left a Book of Mormon with someone at the house. Before passing out the books, he underlined important passages in the book about reading and praying to know the truth, and he always included contact information in case they wanted to know more. Elder Musungu trusted that anybody who was prepared and ready to hear the gospel would find those passages in the Book of Mormon and begin their own journey, just as he had.

Elder Musungu continued to share the message that had changed his life to hundreds of people throughout the Kenya Nairobi mission areas. It didn't matter whether someone was a high-ranking leader of government or living a life of poverty. He knew the message had the potential to bring happiness and peace to all, and Elder Musungu worked his hardest to share the good news. Whether speaking in English or Swahili, his heart and soul were open, and the people felt it. Hundreds were touched and intrigued by his testimony.

Amram sat with a sea of investigators and other missionaries at the small branch in Tanzania. Together they raised their voices in love and commitment to the Lord as they considered the difference they were making in people's lives. Amram had never felt such joy in his life.

We are sowing, daily sowing
Countless seeds of good and ill,
Scattered on the level lowland,
Cast upon the windy hill;
Seeds that sink in rich, brown furrows,
Soft with heaven's gracious rain;
Seeds that rest upon the surface
Of the dry, unyielding plain;

Thou who knowest all our weakness,
Leave us not to sow alone!
Bid thine angels guard the furrows
Where the precious grain is sown,
Till the fields are crown'd with glory,
Filled with mellow, ripened ears,
Filled with fruit of life eternal
From the seed we sowed in tears.

. . .

Amram's feet were motionless as he stood on the dirt road leading to his village, but his heart was racing with anticipation. He had just finished an eight-hour bus ride from Nairobi to an area close to Hamuyundi. The bus bumped along the roads all night long, which hadn't allowed much sleep. Not that Amram could have slept much anyway. He had given away five copies of the Book of Mormon and ten Joseph Smith Testimony pamphlets to the bus driver and various passengers.

Amram prayed silently that those on the bus who were willing to talk to him about the gospel had felt the Spirit and would be inspired to learn more. The bus driver had been persuaded by Amram to play the Tabernacle Choir CD he carried with him. The voices of the choir testified through hymns of the Restoration and filled the dark bus with beautiful music of light and God's love. The choir brought every emotion to the surface for Amram, and he never tired of listening to them.

Finally able to stretch his legs, Amram attempted to brush the wrinkles out of his clothing from the long journey. He squared his shoulders, proudly lifted his head, and took the first step toward home in three years. His parents would be so surprised to see him. There had been no way for him to tell them he was coming.

When President Brown was released from the Kenya Nairobi Mission, he was replaced by President Clark. Amram had been inspired by both great men and was determined to model his life after them. When President Clark released Amram from his full-time missionary service, he had instructed him to go home and see his family in the village for a few days. Amram had reunited with his brother in the Kibera slum in Nairobi for two days before finding a bus that would take him to the village where his parents lived. Now his eyes took in the familiar surroundings. It was just a three-mile walk down the dirt road to his village. Finally, this day he had been expecting for so long had come.

Amram was a changed man on both the inside and outside. He had come to love dressing like a missionary, so he wore his white shirt, tie, suit, and a well-worn pair of missionary shoes. It represented all that Amram had been doing and how he still felt in his heart. He hoped his parents would be proud.

As Amram continued on the journey home, he suddenly recognized a young man walking toward him. It was a friend from school years ago who had almost walked right past him on the road. Clearly, he didn't recognize Amram.

"Hello! It's Am." *Am* was a shortened nickname friends and family in the village often used.

The friend turned to face Amram with wide eyes. "Wow! You're back. I didn't even know it was you! When I saw you, I figured you were some government official or something."

Amram laughed, and they exchanged a quick conversation before Amram turned to continue his journey home.

"Hey, I just saw your mom in the village on my way up. I bet she's going to be excited to see you."

Amram nodded in agreement and waved as he picked up the pace. He was getting closer. Beautiful memories of home began to flood his consciousness, and strong emotions rose to the surface.

Oh, how I've missed my mom.

As his footsteps quickened to where the dirt road continued down a hill, the small village came into view. From the distance, he could see a woman on the outskirts of the village. Could it be his mother? Amram squinted his eyes and focused on the woman. *It was her!* He saw his mother look up in his direction then lower her head. Amram smiled.

She doesn't recognize me. I'm not the barefoot boy who left this village.

"Mom!" Amram yelled.

Her head came up with a jerk, and her wide eyes barely blinked as they tried to focus on the figure in the distance.

"It's me . . . Amram!"

Amram's mother began to run. Joyful sobs escaped her lips as her feet rushed up the path to greet her son. Amram bounded forward several steps to close the distance between them then opened his arms. He grabbed onto his mother and wrapped his arms tightly around her neck. Together they stood and wept.

Amram had never hugged his mother before. In accordance with the culture of the village, appreciation was voiced, but hugs were not given. Amram experienced hugs for the first time while on his mission, and he had a strong desire to express his love that way to his parents.

"Look at you, Am!" Mother exclaimed. She grabbed his face in her hands, recognizing her young son's features in the now young man's face. "Come now! Your father is home. You must see him."

Amram walked in the door to the hut and saw his father. Amram wrapped his arms around his father's broad shoulders and pulled him in for a long hug.

"What a great surprise! It looks like Tanzania was good to you, Amram," Father said.

"I did what you asked, and I worked very hard," Amram replied. They both smiled at the memory of their last visit two years earlier at the missionary apartment he shared with Elder Thomas.

Amram's return was a joyous reunion, and word spread quickly that he was back in the village for a few days after living away for three years. Siblings and grandchildren along with neighbors and friends gathered to hear about Amram's journey. All eyes and ears were fixed as Amram began.

"I was a missionary for The Church of Jesus Christ of Latter-Day Saints. The Church has just now come to Nairobi, but I hope someday it will be here in this village. Young men and women can prepare themselves to go and serve a mission to teach people about Jesus Christ. They are called by a prophet who lives in the United States of America at the headquarters of the Church. A short time after I joined the Church, they asked me to be a missionary. It has been the greatest joy of my life to teach the gospel and serve people."

"How did you join the Church?" his mother asked.

"I was baptized in the water, just like it was in the Pentecostal Church," Amram replied.

"I thought you could be baptized only once," his mother stated.

"Yes, but it must be with the right authority," Amram explained.

"Look at my son. He is a preacher and a very good man," Amram's father stated. "We need to have a special meal for our special visitor."

A chicken was slaughtered and cooked along with cornmeal. Together as a family, they feasted as Amram continued to tell stories and help them understand what he had been doing as a missionary. They listened eagerly as Amram shared his testimony and taught them about the gospel. Amram's heart and stomach were full, but there was one more visit Amram needed to make today. And it couldn't wait.

. . .

"Grandma, it's me—Am."

Her frail body lay in the corner of the mud hut down the road from Amram's parents' hut. Amram kneeled beside her, grateful and amazed that she was still alive. The family had sent messages to Amram several times on his mission that she was close to death. She was now 107 years old and could not move or function on her own anymore.

"Grandma, I've come back to see you," Amram said, squeezing her hand. She forced a quiet smile and peered out of half-closed eyes at her grandson. This grandson had been given the name of her husband—Musungu. *Amram* was a biblical name and belonged to Moses's father. Amram's parents loved the symbolism of the great man mentioned in the book of Exodus in the Old Testament, and they had given him the name as his first name. It was an honor to carry both his grandfather's name of Musungu and the biblical name of Amram.

Amram's heart was heavy. The many years had taken their toll on his grandmother's body. She had been such a beautiful example of strength and courage throughout her life. Her name, *Rebeccah*, was spelled exactly as found in the bible. His grandmother had loved God throughout her life just as the biblical woman in the scriptures had done.

"Grandma, I want to give you a priesthood blessing," Amram whispered. "A blessing of comfort."

Amram placed his hands on his grandmother's head and paused for a moment. How would he begin?

Heavenly Father understands everything.

He began to pray in English. Because of his time as a missionary, the specific terms used in the blessing were easier for him to speak in English than his native Swahili. Amram wanted Heavenly Father to act on her behalf according to His will. He asked if she could go peacefully and not stay any longer in mortality to suffer. Tears of faith fell silently down Amram's cheeks.

Following the blessing, Amram sat quietly next to his grandmother. He recognized the significance of the event. What a privilege to hold the priesthood. He was certain this blessing was the first of its kind in the small village. The people here had no understanding of the authority of the priesthood or the miracles and blessings that came with it. Amram reached over and squeezed her hand one final time before turning to leave.

Amram's grandmother died peacefully an hour later.

THE CHURCH OF JESUS CHRIST OF LATTER-DAY SAINTS
KENYA NAIROBI MISSION

Inorero House, Forest Road, P.O. Box 39634 Nairobi, Kenya, Telephone: 011 254 2 740 - 444 Fax: 011 254 2 740 - 222 East - Africa

29 August 1995

Dear Elder Musungu,

I want to congratulate you on the completion of a most honorable mission. You have served our Father in Heaven valiantly. You have been faithful to your commitment. You are been diligent in carrying out your assignment.

You have served with a singleness of purpose that has won my admiration and respect. I have watched closely as you have taught, lead and given support to your brother missionaries. I have been impressed with your knowledge of the gospel. I have been aware of the many people whom you have brought to a knowledge of the truthfulness of this church. You have blessed many of the children of God as you have brought souls unto Christ.

You have served without murmuring, even though the circumstances have been difficult and the challenges many. I want to thank you for sustaining me as your leader. You will be a great strength to the church all you life if you will continue giving the same kind of service that you have rendered during this two year mission.

The Lord Himself has accepted your efforts and He is pleased with your service. You have served Him with a dedicated heart and an eye single to His glory.

It is my prayer that you will continue throughout your lives to serve with the same dedication of heart, might mind and strength to build up the Kingdom of God on Earth. May you so do I pray and I leave you my blessings as your president with heartfelt love for you. Remember all you days that
I sure love you,

Sincerely,

Paul Kenneth Clark, President

Elder Musungu and Elder Price teaching a family in Tanzania.

Amram with President and Sister Clark in the mission field.

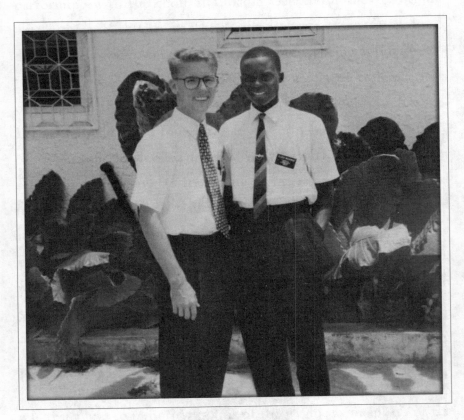

Elder Price and Elder Musungu

CHAPTER SIX

Never, never, never postpone following a prompting.

Thomas S. Monson

"I am here to collect my passport."

Amram had been to the passport office at the Kenyan Immigration Office every Monday through Friday for three months to check on the progress of his passport. It was supposed to be a two-week process, but there were always more hoops to jump through in Kenya. Corruption was certain.

"I have a letter here to attend college in the United States. I must have a passport," Amram declared.

On his mission, Amram's companions from the United States talked about the colleges and universities in Utah and Idaho. Just hearing about the programs offered at the schools ignited a strong desire in Amram to study abroad in the United States. Perhaps if he could get an education and be successful, then one day he might help his village be more successful.

After Amram's mission, he studied hard and passed the TOEFL exam, which was designed to test the English language skills of foreign students wishing to attend an English-speaking university. His mission president, Paul Clark, had even helped him submit the applications. Because Amram had spent his life running miles as his own form of transportation, President Clark had a missionary time him on a track, and they submitted those times in an attached letter with the hope that a school might give him a track scholarship. A university track team was not in Amram's future, but he did receive an acceptance letter from Ensign College in Utah. Now he needed that passport.

Amram watched closely as the passport officer shuffled through the pile of paperwork with attached passports. Amram caught a glimpse of his name as the officer grabbed the document and slipped it into a drawer. Amram knew what that meant: the officer was looking for a bribe.

Amram offered a silent prayer, trusting that it would be heard. *Dear Heavenly Father, I have good faith that if you want me to go to America, you can make this possible for me.* He had no money for a bribe.

"I need to speak to the head of Immigration," Amram demanded. It was a daunting challenge, and he tried to steady his voice.

Amram was led into a room, where he handed over the college acceptance letter. Amram explained that he needed his passport to travel to the United States, and that he had seen the passport on the officer's desk before it was tucked away.

"Give this young man his passport," the leader snapped. "Immediately!"

The officer opened his drawer, thumbed through a stack of paperwork, and handed the document across the desk to Amram.

It was an answered prayer that moved Amram one step closer to his dream.

. . .

No personal bank account. No wealthy family members. No job.

Amram noticed the amount of blank space on his own visa application and rubbed his forehead. The prospects for securing a visa at the American Embassy in Kenya were grim under the best circumstances. Plenty of encouragement came from Johnson Mwaura, who was the elder's quorum president in Kibera; Amram was serving as his first counselor. Even with Johnson's moral support, Amram understood that chances were slim, but he was determined to cling to his faith. If God wanted him in the United States, a door would open. The door might be very small and might be barely cracked open, but that door was somewhere. Amram knew he needed to do his part by giving his best effort and never giving up hope.

Amram knelt by his bed in the shanty he shared with his brother. He was grateful to be back in Kibera attending the branch there and continuing to assist the missionary effort. But something in his heart told him there was more. Tomorrow morning, he would walk the ten miles to the embassy to apply for a visa.

"Dear Heavenly Father, I'm grateful for this great life. My family. For blessings that this gospel has brought to my life. To have served my mission. . . ."

Thoughts of tomorrow's events overwhelmed his senses as he prayed. Amram had taught families on his mission about replacing fear with faith. He desperately needed to follow his own counsel but was humbled by the enormity of it all. Amram continued in his prayerful request.

". . . and maybe I can get an education and continue to do missionary work in the United States." Amram paused then continued with a request that came from deep inside his soul.

"Please build a bridge for me to cross over to this country. Heavenly Father . . . I need a bridge."

Suddenly, Amram heard a quiet thought. *Go see Jackson Ehaji.*

Jackson was a friend who lived in the Kibera slums with his siblings and had also served as a missionary at the same time as Amram. *Go see Jackson?* It was evening, but not too late to pay a visit to his friend's shanty. Amram jumped to his feet and took the necessary shortcuts through the slum to his friend's place.

"Jackson, do you have a minute?"

"Sure, Am. Good to see you."

"Tomorrow morning, I'm going to the American embassy to apply for a visa. I don't have everything, but I have faith. I have a testimony of a living God of miracles. I have my school papers, my passport, and I have an acceptance letter from Ensign College."

The two locked eyes. They both understood that a visa was a significant hurdle.

"Jackson, I know that God knows what I'm going through right now. I can feel it."

"How about I give you a priesthood blessing, Amram? I can do it right here in this room," Jackson suggested.

"Thank you, Jackson," Amram said. "I appreciate that."

That evening two poor, young men who understood the blessings of the priesthood came together to ask for a miracle. In simple surroundings, a faithful voice reached upward with a momentous request for his friend. In the darkness of the Kibera slum, the shanty was a tender, holy space of light and hope. With heads bowed in the humble setting, both knew they needed a bridge of miracles.

. . .

Amram woke early with the sun, walked the ten-mile distance, and arrived in downtown Nairobi to find a long line outside the American embassy. He took his place in line and watched as people talked about securing their own visa. Many had bank statements showing financial security. Amram had only a passport and the faith that God would provide a miracle.

The line eventually moved up until they were finally inside the building. Over and over, people were turned away from the visa counselor in tears. A rejection meant you were required to wait for one year before you were permitted to try again. It was disheartening for Amram to watch people's dreams dashed away in an instant. Soon the mood for those standing in line switched from excited anticipation to solemnity and doubt.

One specific visa counselor was turning everybody down and appeared to relish the consistent slam of the decline stamp on all paperwork presented. Repeatedly Amram watched as people turned and walked away in tears. There was a woman in front of Amram whose turn became available, and she saw the feared counselor's window was open. She twirled around to face Amram.

"You can go. There is something else I need to do," she groaned as she stepped off to the side.

"Next!" shouted the visa counselor.

Amram swallowed hard and took the few steps required to approach the window. It felt like the longest walk of his life. He forced a look of confidence on his face and handed the counselor his paperwork. The counselor reviewed the form then looked up at Amram for several seconds.

"Young man, when you go to the United States, I would ask you to go to a four-year university and get your education. We will keep your passport here and will stamp the visa. Come back at 4:00 p.m. and pay fifty dollars to collect your passport and visa. Good luck with your studies in the United States."

It took a few moments for Amram to comprehend the counselor's response. His heart was pounding so loudly, he wondered if he had heard correctly. The counselor looked past

Amram at the next person in line, indicating the transaction was complete. Amram quickly walked across the room but couldn't leave—not yet. He leaned up against the wall at the back of the building so that his legs could catch up with his pounding heart.

What just happened here? This is a miracle from God.

Most of the people in the room were crying now. People's applications were rejected one after another. Amram watched the scene in front of him for fifteen minutes while mixed feelings of overwhelming joy and disbelief consumed his thoughts.

I am just a poor boy, but God sees me.

Amram turned and walked out the door of the embassy to distance himself from the cries of disappointment and sorrow so many were feeling. He moved quickly to leave the crowds surrounding the embassy before allowing the smile on his face to emerge. With it came an overwhelming joy in Amram's heart. He thought back to the priesthood blessing given the night before. Two humble brothers from the Kibera Branch had trusted in the Lord in great faith.

There was still a challenge ahead. Amram did not have the fifty dollars required to pick up the visa. *God has given me the miracle of the visa, so surely I will find a way to get the fifty dollars.*

Amram turned on his heel and began the ten-mile walk back to the slum. The prayer in his heart came in the form of a song. The lyrics and melody burst out of Amram's lungs in gratitude and love as he walked the streets of Nairobi, singing loudly with tears streaming down his face.

> *We thank thee, O God, for a prophet*
> *To guide us in these latter days.*
> *We thank thee for sending the gospel*
> *To lighten our minds with its rays.*
> *We thank thee for every blessing*
> *Bestowed by thy bounteous hand.*
> *We feel it a pleasure to serve thee*
> *And love to obey thy command.*

Amram continued to vocalize the prayer as he felt the meaning of the song. He had made a commitment to sustain the prophet of the Lord and trusted that if he continued in the gospel, the Lord would help and bless him. He had never met the prophet, but just seeing him on television during conference sessions was a powerful testimony. The hymn had always been a favorite of his, and Amram especially loved hearing the Tabernacle Choir sing it. Today, as he sang and continued his journey home, it took on an even deeper meaning.

. . .

Fifty dollars in Kenya was a lot of money for a poor young man. It had been two days since the visa was ready, but Amram had been unable to find work or anybody else who could lend him the money. He wondered if the embassy would assume that he was just a poor guy who would be a burden to America. Amram continued to pray for help.

The next afternoon, the full-time missionaries from the Kibera Branch stopped by Amram's place to see if he would go out proselyting with them for a few hours. They had with them a young man who wasn't a missionary. He was an American tourist who was visiting Kenya and had just come from a safari adventure in the country and wanted to go out tracting with the missionaries for the afternoon.

"Sure," Amram agreed. "I'll go out with you." He was always willing to work with the missionaries. The fifty-dollar obstacle was heavy on his mind, and he was really beginning to worry because he had not found any new leads. *Perhaps some good missionary work for a couple of hours will lift my spirits.*

Amram introduced himself to the tourist, then turned to address the two missionaries.

"Hey, guys, you know how I want to go to school at Ensign College in Utah? Well, I was blessed with a miracle to get acceptance for the visa a few days ago, but I can't pay the fifty dollars to collect it. I've spent the last two days searching for work to earn the money but can't find anything. I don't know what I'm going to do."

"Fifty dollars?" the tourist interrupted. "You need only fifty dollars?"

63

▲ ▲ ▲ ▲

"Yes," Amram replied. "But fifty dollars is a large sum of money for me."

The tourist pulled out his wallet, counted a few bills, and looked directly at Amram. He extended his hand with fingers holding the counted money toward Amram.

"There you go," the tourist smiled.

"Fifty dollars for your visa."

Elder Ehaji and Elder Musungu in the mission field. Elder Ehaji is the one who gave Amram a priesthood blessing asking for a miracle for the VISA.

CHAPTER SEVEN

It is extremely important for you to believe in yourselves,

not only for what you are now, but for what

you have the power to become.

Trust in the Lord as He leads you along.

He has things for you to do that you won't know about now,

but that will unfold later.

Neal A. Maxwell

"Amram, we have sold a portion of our land. It's not enough to pay for your airline ticket, but it is the best we can do."

Amram looked at the two beautiful people who had reared him well. Now they were sacrificing again to ensure he would have a better life. Their contribution was a fraction of the thousand dollars needed to purchase the ticket, but it meant everything.

"I am so grateful to you both," Amram said. "This means so much to me. I'll find the rest of the money and find a way to get a good education in the United States. I promise to make you proud."

"Some of our friends in the village are helping as well," Amram's mother continued. "They are selling eggs and vegetables from their gardens and setting aside the money for your ticket. We are all pulling for you."

What compassion and kindness. Amram's parents and the villagers could barely make ends meet, and yet they found room to give. This village was poor in money but rich in spirit. Amram felt a deep desire to return to this village one day and make things better for everyone.

. . .

Amram put on his white shirt, tie, and slacks and prepared to walk several miles into the city. Every morning was the same routine. He woke up, dressed his best, and spent the day walking the streets of Nairobi hoping to find someone who could support his education. With a prayer on his lips and persistence in his steps, Amram began again. Perhaps today would be different.

Amram had spent a month going to government offices, ministers of finance, and political offices every single day, but nobody would personally meet with him. He left messages at every office, vowed to return, and continued his search for another.

A few days earlier, he had walked to the home of a United States diplomat who was working in Kenya and knocked on the front door. The diplomat was home and willing to listen as Amram explained his desire to go to college in Utah. This diplomat was kind enough to give a hundred dollars toward the desired education. It was a generous gift, and Amram assured him he would use it wisely.

Although the challenge ahead seemed insurmountable without meaningful employment, Amram refused to give up hope. He still needed hundreds of dollars just to purchase the airline ticket to Utah. He trusted that his prayers would be answered, but he also knew he must try his very best.

Heavenly Father, where should I go? Please guide me to an opportunity. Help me find a bridge to the United States.

Suddenly, Amram had a strong feeling to return to a politician's office that he had already visited numerous times. He had been turned away repeatedly. Amram recognized the prompting and quickly made his way to the office.

Once again, he introduced himself, and the politician heard and recognized the name. He had seen the name again and again on a requested appointment list. Amram explained his situation and the need for a ticket to go to America to begin his studies.

The politician listened to Amram's story with a soft heart. He could see potential in the young man standing in front of him.

"I am certain you will make something of yourself, Mr. Musungu, and an education is a good place to start. I will contribute 50,000 shillings."

That would pay for half the ticket! Amram knew he'd been blessed, and God had heard his plea. Another prompting soon led him to seek out a businessman in the sugar industry who listened to Amram's desire to make a better life for himself. He also gave a generous contribution.

Amram carefully counted the money. Between the diplomat, politician, land sale from his family, and a few coins from the villagers, Amram believed he had enough to purchase an airline ticket from Kenya to Utah. He ran to the travel office and purchased the ticket.

Amram held the one-way ticket to his heart and placed the leftover fifty dollars in his pocket.

. . .

Fifty dollars.

Amram reached deep into his pocket and felt again for the folded bills. It was all he had left, and it would have to be enough. Fifty dollars, his missionary scriptures, his missionary journal, and a small bag with a change of clothes were everything he owned temporally, but spiritually he had the Lord on his side, and that meant everything.

What a year it had been since returning home from his mission. Amram saw and felt lessons and miracles during the twenty-seven months of his mission, but he had witnessed new miracles since then that brought him to this point. It was a humbling experience to look at his visa and remember the scene of tears and devastation that had befallen so many at the embassy. He trusted God would continue to lift him up and open doors for great opportunities in the United States. Amram possessed grit and determination, but more than that, he trusted God implicitly.

The announcement for his flight blared throughout the airport halls. Amram's stomach twisted in nervous anticipation and excitement with a range of emotions racing and fighting for control. He had never been on an airplane or left the African continent before. Amram took a deep breath and let it out slowly. He bowed his head silently before boarding the flight. The events of the past year could not be explained. Amram knew he had been carried.

Thank you, dear Heavenly Father, for building a bridge.

.   .   .

"Ladies and gentlemen, we will be landing shortly in Belgium."

Amram closed the scriptures he had been reading during most of the eight-hour flight. He quickly tucked them in the small bag under the seat in front of him. It would be another flight from Belgium to Ohio in the United States and then finally to Utah. Reading the scriptures had been an intentional choice so he could feel the peace and love of the Savior, and Amram was grateful. But it didn't provide any answers to new burning questions.

Where will I stay? What does life look like in this new country?

Fifty dollars was a lot of money in Kenya, but Amram knew it wouldn't last long in the United States. But that meager amount combined with his faith would have to be enough. Amram had seen miracles before and didn't doubt.

Amram grabbed his simple belongings and disembarked the flight to find himself in the international airport in Belgium. There he discovered a long delay for the next connection. The flight attendants alerted the passengers to the details of the delay and explained they could use the telephone to notify those picking them up at the airport. It was a reminder to Amram that he was alone in this journey.

Suddenly, he was impressed to look in his missionary journal. Thumbing through the pages, he saw the phone number of a missionary couple from Utah who had served in Kenya with him. They were a wonderful older couple in their seventies who had developed a good relationship with Amram, and they had given him their number hoping they could keep in touch.

"How can I make an international call?" Amram asked the airport employee.

"You are a passenger on the delayed flight? Yes, use this phone over here."

Amram dialed the phone number and waited for the connection. He heard one ring, then two. Finally, the phone call was answered.

"Hello, this is Elder Musungu. You remember—from the Kenya Mission?"

"Of course, Elder Musungu! How great to hear from you. Where are you calling from?"

"I am calling from the airport in Belgium, but I'm eventually coming to Salt Lake City airport. I don't have much time to talk, but I was hoping you would be willing to pick me up from the airport and help find me a place to stay for a few days until I get an apartment. I have been accepted to Ensign College."

"Wow! Congratulations! Yes, we can pick you up at the airport. We'll help you figure this out, Elder Musungu, and we can talk later. Tell me the time your flight is supposed to arrive."

Amram quickly supplied the arrival time, hung up the phone, and felt a wave of love and gratitude for the kind couple and the opportunity he'd had to meet them in Kenya. What were the chances he had written their phone number in his journal two years earlier? It was another testament that God's hand had been directing Amram's path for some time.

. . .

There they stood. What a beautiful sight to see this generous missionary couple grinning and waving. Amram's body was tired from the long trip, but his spirit soared when he saw them outside the arrival gates.

Hugs were exchanged and then a jacket was held up. "Wait until you get outside this airport. You're in for a surprise, so we brought this for you."

It was December 12, 1997, and winters in Utah were in stark contrast to those in Kenya. They walked through the airport toward the main exit leading to the parking garage. Amram noticed that everyone was wearing coats. Soon enough the exit doors opened, and a blast of icy wind rushed inside to welcome Amram to his new world. He quickly slid the jacket on, grateful these kind people had thought to bring it to him.

Snow. Amram had read about it and seen it on television, but it was a crazy sensation to see and feel it for himself. What a new world! Amram braced himself for some real change that went way beyond the weather. The sights and sounds in the airport environment alone were an explosion in strangeness. It was both thrilling and intimidating.

The missionary couple told Amram he could stay in their basement until he figured out some permanent housing. As they drove to the house, they all discussed what had been happening in Kenya since the couple had left the mission. It was a joyful reunion of laughter as fond memories were shared between the three of them.

After Amram's first dinner in the United States, he excused himself to retire for the evening. It felt like days since he had slept. Before he lay his tired head on the pillow, he knelt by his bed for the first time in the United States. What a difference this bed was from the banana leaves on the floor of his brother's shanty. That world felt so far away.

"Heavenly Father, this has been a journey of good faith. You have been in everything I have ever done in my life. Your influence has touched everything." Amram's mind considered the passport, visa, airfare money, and love of his family who desperately wanted his dreams to come true. The pattern of miracles was certain, and Amram continued his humble prayer. "I did not come here by chance, and I know that. I promise to work hard."

Amram's soft heart was fully committed.

"I believe you need me here."

. . .

"You must pay your tuition."

The International Student Advisor at Ensign College had just stamped Amram's foreign student papers and finished informing Amram of all instructions pertaining to the school and his class registration. Then came the final request for money.

Amram stared at the advisor and swallowed hard.

"I don't have anything, but I'm willing to work," Amram replied. He sat up straight in his chair.

"You don't have any money?" the advisor confirmed.

"No, Sir," Amram stated, "but I can do any work."

The advisor looked across the desk at the courageous young man sitting there. Africa? There was surely a story behind this young man's journey and ability to get to the United States.

"We have a custodial job that pays $5.50 an hour for twenty hours a week. You'll need to make payments to your tuition account."

"Yes, I'll take that job," Amram said. "Thank you so much."

. . .

"You need to have a password," the professor instructed, "and that password should be something you can remember."

Amram was determined to study computer science, and it would all begin in this Introduction to Computer Information Systems class, but Amram had never touched a computer before in his life. Amram quickly wrote down the instruction then watched as the other students began to type. His wide eyes and blank stare caught the attention of the student sitting next to him.

"You know what—just do this," the student demonstrated. "Now type your name as your password."

Amram obediently punched the letters of his name next to the blinking prompt, and that was the start of Amram's education in the United States. He worked the part-time job, diligently studied for high grades in every class, and eventually found an apartment. His own two feet and the city bus system supplied all necessary transportation. There were many days of surviving on bread and oranges. It wasn't much, but the meager meal did give Amram the strength to focus on his studies and to clean the school.

In two years, Amram graduated with three associate degrees and an accounting certificate. He continued his studies at Westminster College and later earned a master's degree in accounting. Throughout his educational experience, Amram never lost sight of who he was, where he was going, and the miracles that brought him to the United States. He threw himself into missionary work in the Salt Lake City area by tagging along with the missionaries who were serving in the area. There in quiet homes he could testify of God providing the way for a poor, barefoot boy.

Little did Amram know that there were still bridges ahead that would pull his voice into the world.

Amram (top right) at graduation in 1999 with Accounting/Computer Science degrees.

KENYA

Figure 5
Tribesman gazing at the Kenyan landscape.

CHAPTER EIGHT

True enduring happiness with the accompanying strength,

courage, and capacity to overcome the most challenging difficulties

comes from a life centered in Jesus Christ.

Richard G. Scott

Amram sat on the edge of his bed staring into the empty space, as if the answers were clearly visible there. Amram understood that Heavenly Father had blessed him with tools he needed to move forward, but this was something he had never seen coming. Never thought about it. Never planned it.

The letter Amram had just received was still tightly clutched in his fingers. He folded the paper and placed it back into the envelope only to pull it out again and reread the first paragraph. The mantle felt heavy on his shoulders as he contemplated what would be required of him. Amram would do anything for missionary work, but this was a way to serve that he had never imagined.

Amram's heart pounded as he considered the courage and discipline he would need to embrace this new opportunity.

Amram's feet picked up the pace in order to make the next ride. A stroke of luck and his quick strides launched him inside the elevator at the Church Office Building in Salt Lake City just before the doors closed. It was a beautiful spring day in 2002, and Amram had found a new job working in the Finance Department for The Church of Jesus Christ of Latter-day Saints. His continuing education was already blessing his life, and he was grateful for another job to make ends meet.

"Wow, just in time," Amram said to the people gathered inside. He nodded at the others and smiled. "It's a good morning."

Amram noticed one gentleman who looked familiar.

Is that Craig Jessop?

He had seen him just the morning before while attending a Sunday morning program called *Music and The Spoken Word* where the Tabernacle Choir performed. Craig Jessop was one of the choir conductors. Amram often went to see the Sunday performances to fill the void of music he so missed from his upbringing. The music filled his soul like it did when his father conducted small neighborhood and church choirs in Kenya. It was also a sweet reminder of his time on his mission. So often the missionaries played the Tabernacle Choir CDs to fill the apartment with words of enlightenment and beauty.

One by one the others got off the elevator on various floors. Finally, only Amram and Craig Jessop remained. Amram was remembering they had exchanged greetings on several occasions in the elevator. He wondered what business he might have in this building.

"Can I ask you something?" Craig asked. "I would love for you to come and visit with me in my office on the twenty-first floor for a few minutes. You seem to have a good, beautiful voice."

Amram was surprised by the request. Maybe he wanted to be friends.

"Okay, sure," Amram replied. "I have a little time this afternoon."

After work, Amram took the elevator from his office on the seventeenth floor and continued up four floors to meet Craig Jessop. When he walked onto the floor, Amram saw a sign on the door stating that these were the offices for the Tabernacle Choir. Craig welcomed Amram, introductions were made to the staff and secretaries, then Craig turned and looked directly at Amram.

"Amram, can you sing?"

"Sure, I can sing. I've been singing all my life."

"Okay, come with me."

Amram followed Craig down the hall to another large room where there was a piano. He wondered where this was leading. Craig picked up a hymnbook and handed it to Amram.

"Pick one of your favorite songs."

What is happening? This guy has access to all kinds of talent, but maybe he just loves music and wants to hear me sing.

Amram quickly thumbed through the pages until he found a hymn that had great meaning. The words had always motivated him on his mission. The theme of a beautiful work, missionary zeal, and learning to appreciate people filled Amram's soul whenever he sang the lyrics. He showed the page to Craig, who positioned himself at the piano. Craig began to play, and Amram's low, bass voice filled the room with a melodious testimony.

Sweet is the work, my God, my King,
To praise thy name, give thanks and sing,
To show thy love by morning light,
And talk of all thy truths at night.

Amram was close to the end of the final verse when Craig stopped.

"Have you ever thought of auditioning for the Tabernacle Choir?" Craig asked.

"No," Amram answered.

Amram didn't even hesitate in answering. The thought had truly never crossed his mind. In addition to working a few part-time jobs, Amram was still in college taking eighteen credit hours and striving for higher educational degrees.

"Well, you have a very beautiful voice, Amram. I ask you to go home, pray about it, and come back to me and tell me what you think," Craig said.

"Sure, I can do that," Amram said quietly.

This choir is filled with professionally trained people, and I'm just a poor guy who loves music and sings by ear.

Amram tried to hide the apprehension building in his chest.

And I don't see any other black people in that choir.

. . .

A bead of sweat slowly trickled down the side of Amram's face. He reached up and quickly swiped it away before it dropped from his jaw. Amram could feel the heat rising up his neck into his face and ears and knew he was sweating profusely. This was way out of his comfort zone.

"Just take a break for one minute," Craig said. "Take a deep breath and relax—everything will be fine." It was obvious to the director that Amram's nerves were getting the best of him.

The final step of the audition was an oral test in the Tabernacle—singing a selected piece of music for Tabernacle Choir conductors Craig Jessop and Mack Wilberg with an organist accompanying the music. Amram agreed to audition for the choir after considering that God might be putting him in a place where Amram's example could reach beyond his individual ability. Perhaps this was an unexpected teaching opportunity that God had intentionally placed in Amram's path. In a humble prayer, he had agreed to place himself in that path with his own commitment of effort.

There had been months of arduous studies and testing levels to pass before getting to this point. Amram did his best to try to learn musical theory on the internet and in the choir school that he attended all summer. It was another sacrifice of time from a schedule already full with the demands of work and school. With no car, the bus was his only reliable transportation.

Amram stepped up to the music stand and confirmed his readiness to the organist. He looked up at Craig, who nodded his head in encouragement. With a prayer in his heart, Amram lifted his voice up and sang with the same spirit he had felt his entire life. His love of music and testimony of the gospel poured from his soul just as it had when he was a boy singing in the village church. He loved the memories of singing at home with his father.

Years of singing his devotion to God.

.   .   .

You have been accepted as a member of the Tabernacle Choir.
The statement at the top of the letter took Amram's breath away as his eyes caught sight of it again. His eyes continued down the body of the letter and then stopped. *This is a calling from the prophet as advisor to the choir. You will be set apart as a missionary for The Church of Jesus Christ of Latter-Day Saints.* Requirements were listed regarding rehearsals on Thursdays, Saturdays, and early Sunday mornings. Travel was required for some performances.

Amram pondered the heavy load required but recognized what his example might mean to the world. He would be the first African native to sing in the Tabernacle Choir. It was a responsibility that

Amram felt as he imagined people from Africa and all over the world watching the choir sing.

I will be a representative of the Church and of the love God has for all His children. He sees every single one of us.

Amram tried to push aside the worries of scheduling and financial woes. The city bus schedule would be his lifeline to practices and performances. With this new commitment, he would have to reduce his workload and survive on less money. As Amram had witnessed so many times in his life, a path was always cleared when obstacles or opportunities felt overwhelming. Once again, he would need the Lord's help on another unexpected journey.

· · ·

Glorious.

The word came to Amram's mind as he stood singing with the Tabernacle Choir for the first time. To be enveloped in such sound stirred his senses and elevated his soul to new heights. Sitting a short distance behind President Hinkley and the general leadership of the Church during general conference was exhilarating as Amram sang gospel truths with the choir. Amram, once a young man listening to a CD of what this amazing choir could produce, was now surrounded by the heavenly sounds that had built and inspired the deepest part of his testimony. Tears filled Amram's eyes as he stood with the choir and gave his best effort to sing words of love and gratitude toward God for everything good that had come into his life.

Amram quickly understood why this choir's performances were so flawless and soulful. The impressive dedication required by all members of the choir coupled with their love for the gospel enabled them to sing at a supreme level. This choir had won scores of awards, sold millions of recordings, and enthralled audiences in dozens of countries.

As Amram traveled with them on tours throughout the United States and Canada, his presence in the choir began to get attention. Friends from South Africa emailed to say that families watched closely during general conference and other televised performances to catch sight of the first African to sing with the choir. Parents in Africa pointed Amram out and told their children they could aspire to great things just like him. People from all parts of Africa thanked Amram for representing them well and for reminding them they were a part of this great worldwide church. Newspapers and magazines began requesting interviews with Amram to learn about his conversion, his journey to the United States, and how that led to the choir.

Amram was certainly getting noticed.

. . .

Wait—I know that face. I can't believe it! That's Musungu!

Russell Price was holding a copy of *The Ensign*, a Church magazine mailed to his home each month containing inspirational articles teaching the gospel of Jesus Christ. He blinked hard, then looked again at the photo. It was definitely Amram Musungu, the first baptism of Russell's mission and his last companion in Tanzania. After serving his two-year mission, Russell had returned to his home in Arizona and had lost touch with Elder Musungu.

Russell turned to his family. "I baptized this guy!" he said. "And now he sings in the Tabernacle Choir? I didn't even know he was in the United States!"

Russell scanned the article, which mentioned Amram's journey to the United States and his recent membership in the choir. He quickly looked up the author of the article and sent an email with his own contact information and a request to forward it to Amram. It had been so many years.

After Russell and Amram connected over the phone, Russell brought his family to Utah and made time to sit down and visit Amram. Stories were shared as the two companions caught up on each other's lives. Amram testified of the miracles that had brought him to this point in his life and the missionary work he was still doing in Utah. Russell listened in awe to Amram. Once a barefoot boy on fire with a new testimony, he was now continuing years later to use his miraculous story to share the gospel in multiple ways. The light that emitted from this man's deep-rooted missionary spirit was inspirational.

All future broadcasts of the Tabernacle Choir in the Russell Price home were met with cheers and the joy of one former missionary watching for a glimpse of one he'd baptized so many years ago. Russell never tired of making the declaration.

"That's my guy."

"Wow, I didn't know there were black people in your church."

Amram turned and smiled at the gentleman. He was performing with the choir at Lincoln Center for the Performing Arts in New York City and had walked outside for a quick break during a rehearsal. Amram was getting used to being approached.

"Oh, yes," Amram responded, "there are entire congregations of people in this church all over the world that look just like me. Let me tell you how I found it."

This mission looked drastically different from the one Amram served in Africa, but his testimony was the same. People stopped him after performances wanting to know his story. He continued to receive letters from people whose lives he had touched just by his membership in the choir. Nellie, a woman in Cedar City, Utah, wrote to Amram saying she was greatly touched by watching him sing and knowing that the Church was a global and diverse church. She was in her nineties and had waited a long time to feel that spiritual affirmation.

Amram appeared at events to share his experience, whether it was testifying to minority groups of their value as members of the Church or singing "Silent Night" in Swahili at Christmas time. The sacrifice of time and effort for Amram helped him understand and trust this new calling of missionary work. His actions and words declared that "when we sacrifice, we can accomplish great things," and his message rang true to every audience.

For twelve years, Amram testified with his voice in the Tabernacle Choir. He came to know and recognize that his small effort in the choir was supporting the Lord and contributing toward the building of His Church. Amram saw it in people's faces at performances. Read it in so many personal letters received. And felt it within the music.

Amram performing with the Tabernacle Choir at Boise State University in 2005.

Amram on tour with the Tabernacle Choir in New York City.

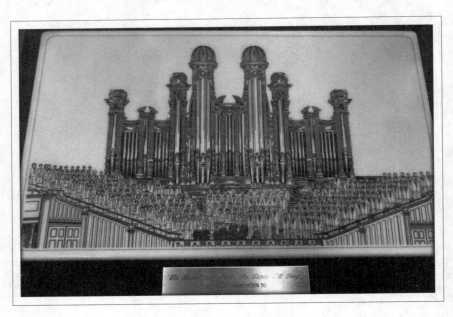

Tabernacle Choir honorary plaque given to Amram.

CHAPTER NINE

Aim at Heaven and you will get Earth thrown in.

Aim at Earth and you will get neither.

C.S. Lewis

"Can I invite my friend? She's studying biology at the University of Utah."

"Sure," Amram answered. "This is a celebration! You can invite anybody—as long as they bring gifts."

"So, the graduate is also a comedian," Amram's friend laughed. "Okay, let's drive together down to Sandy to pick her up."

It was a gathering of friends coming together to celebrate Amram's graduation from Westminster College in the spring of 2002. Just more than four years ago, Amram's wide eyes peered out the airplane window for a first glimpse of his new home. Then those eyes studied computer screens and college textbooks with a strong commitment and drive for a better future. Amram's eyes learned to read music for the first time, which opened the unexpected opportunity to sing praises to huge crowds at performances with the Tabernacle Choir. These past few years, those tear-filled eyes

Amram
You are an inspiration to the
rest of us from Africa who are still struggling
in this great country to accomplish our goals.
Remember back in the day when we were taking classes
together and now you have finished the first leg. I wish
all your dreams come true and all those ambitions put on hold move
a step forward towards accomplishment.
Love Ben

Amram
Congradulation
You are great friend and
I hope the best for
you
You have great future
Mumpta erimbere

Zugenie

Amram's
Graduation

June 8, 2002

Dearest Amram,
    We were so touched
tonight. What a man
of honor you are. I
kept thinking of how
your mother would have
felt if she had been
here tonight. She would
have been so proud &
amazed at all you
have accomplished &
the man you have
become.
    We love being your friend
        Love Rebecca & John

Amram
Congradulation
for your graduation
wish you the best
for your future.

Amram,
    Our paths have crossed briefly
in work and school at the business
college and Westminster. I join
with others as I congradulate you
on this diserved honor.
    Thank you for your example
        Steve Dobb

Page from Amram's graduation booklet.

had continued to testify of God's hand in his life to families living in small apartments throughout the Salt Lake City area who were seeking hope and peace. And those eyes never ceased to look to the heavens and thank God for all recognized blessings. It had been years of sacrifice, but today it was time to celebrate.

Amram's friend turned the car into the driveway of a home located in Sandy and called his friend to announce their arrival. Bright-green growth had filled the trees after a long, cold winter, and tulips and daffodils signaled the observance of spring and seemed to add to the festive mood. Utah winters were not a favorite of Amram's, but the emergence of spring each year was a vision of wonder. It was a welcome break from the snow that had never been a part of African life.

Suddenly, Amram's eyes noticed a beautiful young woman coming out of the house and walking toward their car. Her long, dark hair flowed below her shoulders and cascaded about her blue shirt as she stepped quickly in their direction. When her brown eyes caught sight of the car, she waved a hand and her lips smiled softly. Amram noticed he wasn't breathing. *Wow, is she beautiful.*

"Hi, I'm Noelle," she said after climbing into the car. "Nice to meet you, Amram. Congratulations on your graduation."

"Thank you," Amram said while trying to keep his voice steady. "Glad you can celebrate with us. We're headed to Chinese Gourmet on State Street. The others will meet us there."

"Will your parents be there?" Noelle asked.

"No, they live in Kenya," Amram explained. "I came over in 1997 to get my education."

If she only knew the miracles that brought me here. I'd love to tell her about that sometime.

"Are you planning to head back?" Noelle inquired. She was interested in learning more about this new friend.

"Maybe someday. If God opens a door, I'll walk through it and return to help the people in Kenya. For now, I'm going to continue my education and get a master's degree and pursue some other opportunities here." Amram felt a slight flutter as he considered that *she* might be one of those opportunities.

"How about you, Noelle? How long have you lived in Utah?"

"I was actually born here. My father is from Democratic Republic of Congo, but my mother is from Utah. So, I grew up speaking both French and English." It was obvious she had Amram's full attention. "Do you speak French?"

"Not yet," Amram laughed. "I speak Swahili."

"Well," Noelle smiled. "We'd better stick to English then."

They arrived at Chinese Gourmet, where twelve friends had secured a large table in the back of the restaurant for the celebration. Amram greeted each of them, grateful for their part in his life. He knew these friends from school, church, or other community events. The one thing they all had in common was a respect and admiration for Amram's success, and they were there to show it. The conversation at the table was filled with laughter and joy as they all recalled memories from the past few years.

"Hey, Amram. When you become the President, which office are you going to assign me?" one friend asked.

"Yeah, me too!" another teased. They all laughed, then stared at Amram to hear their individual pronouncements. Amram worked his way around the table and made the assignments as various cabinet and federal government positions.

Amram ran for student body president at Ensign College and made such an impact in his campaign and desire to attain the leadership role to make things better at the school that he had achieved the nickname of *President* among the students and faculty who knew him on campus. The nickname stuck, and many of Amram's friends were certain he would find future leadership roles in the years to come. Amram's positivity and optimistic views were contagious, and he was a natural leader who caught everyone's attention.

"What about me?" Noelle asked. Amram had skipped her. After all, they had met only a couple of hours before. Amram smiled and said the first thing that came to mind.

"How about being the First Lady?" Amram replied.

Everyone roared with laughter, which helped lighten the mood and Amram's sudden realization at what he'd said out loud.

Oh, what did I just say? That's so quick.

. . .

"You know what, Amram? I'd like to meet with the missionaries," Noelle said.

It was a statement Amram had waited to hear for two long years and was an answer to daily heartfelt prayers. The two had struck up a friendship and then dated, but the relationship was conditional. Noelle knew Amram was anxiously engaged in his church and was a member of the Tabernacle Choir, but she wanted nothing to do with his religious affiliations. Her family knew of The Church of Jesus Christ of Latter-day Saints and felt no interest. Early in the relationship, Noelle asked Amram not to tell her about his church. It was a direct challenge to Amram's missionary heart, but he agreed to live the gospel and prayed that the Spirit and his example would speak the words he promised not to vocalize.

"Absolutely. I can arrange that," Amram replied. His heart exploded in silent gratitude. God had heard every single prayer.

A few weeks earlier, Elder M. Russell Ballard asked Amram to meet with him in his office. They had become acquainted through the choir and other missionary endeavors Amram had been involved with in the Salt Lake City area. Amram had brought Noelle along with him to meet the senior Apostle and explained that Elder Ballard held a very high position in church leadership. During that meeting, Elder Ballard had asked her a pivotal question: "Are you a member of the Church, Noelle?"

After some friendly conversation getting to know her, Elder Ballard had reached into a drawer and pulled out a Book of Mormon. He had signed his name inside the front cover and had asked her to go home and read it. Noelle had agreed out of respect for the kind leader. As she began to read, she fell in love with the writings and spirit she felt from the Book of Mormon. Never had she felt so close to her Heavenly Father.

Noelle was excited to learn from the missionaries about living prophets and Apostles who are called of God to lead and guide His Church on the earth today. She was touched to learn about the priesthood used to administer the ordinances of the gospel and to know that Amram would use his own priesthood calling to bless his family. She was inspired by a new eternal perspective of understanding where she lived before she was born and how families could be sealed for eternity. The missionary program and Noelle's vision of future opportunities for temple work brought a new purpose to her life and a sense of peace to her heart.

Weeks of learning with missionary discussions eventually led to Noelle's decision to be baptized by one of the missionaries and to be confirmed to receive the gift of the Holy Ghost by Amram. There had been so many joyous moments in Amram's missionary journeys, but this meant the world to him, and he knew it was another miracle from God to bless his life. Amram and Noelle's love for each other continued to grow throughout the next year as they began to attend church together, to have continuing discussions about the gospel, and to openly share the grace and beauty that spilled into their lives from their commitment to serve others. After a year, Amram knew it was time to take the next step. He felt certain it was right.

I'd better make the first move, or someone else will take her away from me.

. . .

Amram was trembling. He had seen a few proposals on television shows and recognized that the culture here was to get down on one knee. It was different from anything they did in Africa, and he wanted to get it exactly right. Amram had purchased flowers and an engagement ring, but this new cultural expectation of how to do the asking had Amram's nerves getting the best of him.

Amram had excused himself for a moment from their table at The Roof Restaurant in Salt Lake City, and Noelle was sitting at the table by herself. It was a seat by the window overlooking the Salt Lake Temple. The lights against the dark sky illuminated the scene in a way that couldn't have appeared more heavenly. The glowing lights of the temple rose above the glistening city lights. All conditions were perfect, and the rest was up to him.

The manager of the restaurant handed the flowers to Amram after being kind enough to keep them out of sight until the perfect time. Amram felt for the engagement ring in his pocket and fastened it onto a ribbon in the bouquet. Friends had helped him plan the event, but now he was on his own. He wiped the sweat from his forehead and looked over at the manager for encouragement.

"Just go and do it," the manager whispered. "You'll be fine."

Amram took a deep breath and slowly walked toward the table. Activity in the restaurant stopped as customers guessed what was about to happen. Noelle caught sight of him with the flowers and instantly began to cry. The tears caught Amram by surprise.

Wow, what did I do wrong? Why is she crying?

Amram felt all the energy drain from his body and suddenly

felt weak. Instead of dropping down on one knee, he fell to both knees trying to remember if he was getting this right.

Is it one knee or two?

He decided to stay on both knees and handed the flowers to Noelle, told her what she meant to him, then untied the ring from the ribbon in the flowers.

"Noelle, will you be my wife?" Amram asked. It was barely above a whisper, but it was all he could muster in the moment.

The scene sparked a new wave of emotion, and Noelle started crying all over again. Amram felt he might pass out. Noelle used her linen napkin to wipe the tears, then looked directly into Amram's eyes.

"Yes, I will," Noelle cried.

Amram found the strength to climb back onto his feet, and they embraced as future husband and wife. All the staff and diners in the restaurant applauded and cheered for the happy couple. Amram had never felt so relieved and silently grateful that he could lean on Noelle to steady himself and recover a bit. Together their arms enveloped each other in support and love that beautiful winter evening, just as they would for countless years in the future. God had surely brought these two into each other's lives, and the embrace above the spires of the temple was the start of something beautiful.

Months later, on April 15, 2006, Amram and Noelle knelt across an altar in the Salt Lake Temple. The marriage sealing ceremony was performed by M. Russell Ballard and witnessed by Tabernacle Choir director Mac Christensen and Richard P. Lindsay, who was the first Area President for Africa. Amram had met

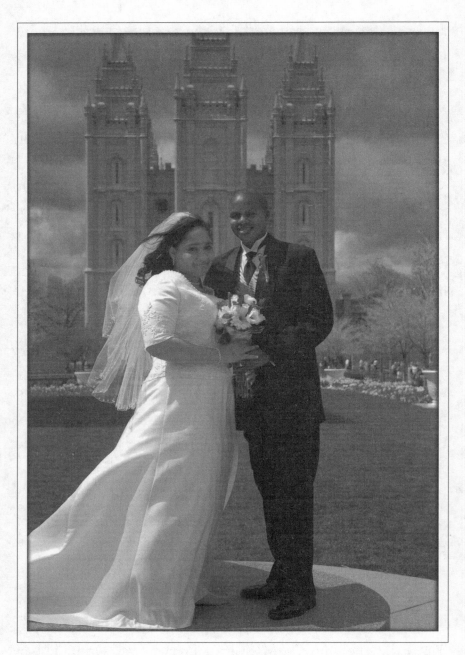

Amram & Noelle wedding day – April 15, 2006, Salt Lake Temple

Elder Lindsay years ago in Kenya when Amram was a new branch mission leader at the age of fourteen. Now these three leaders were there to support this union as mentors and dear friends to Amram. Hopefully, there would be a future day when Amram could introduce his wife to family members in Kenya. How proud they would be of the barefoot boy who had grown up and found both an education and a lovely wife.

Amram's first mission companion, Freddie Thomas, was able to attend the wedding as well, and it was a great reunion for both. In a quiet moment away from the festivities, Freddie pulled a photograph out of his shirt pocket and handed it to Amram. It was the picture taken in their Kibera apartment when Amram's father had come to visit after recovering from malaria. Amram nearly cried out with joy. He had never possessed a picture of his father, so this was a tender keepsake. Amram and Freddie exchanged hugs and a deep appreciation for how their lives had crossed in the past and gratitude for God's hand in both of their lives moving forward.

After friends and family celebrated at a reception for the newlyweds, the sun began its descent below the horizon, creating an array of warm colors that seemed to honor Amram and Noelle's special day. It was a day of two souls uniting in love for each other and God. Two hearts were locked in commitment and purpose. And two ordinary people were destined to come together to make an extraordinary difference in the world.

A future of unforeseen miracles in Amram's life would soon come to pass, but this time those miracles would be manifest with Noelle by his side.

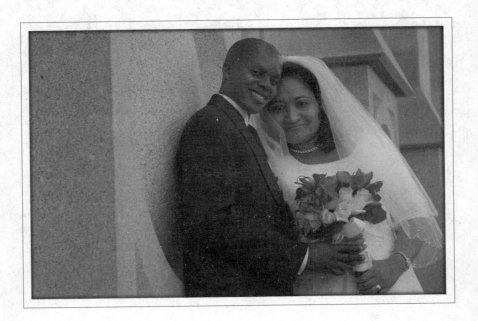

CHAPTER TEN

▲▲▲▲

What counts in life is not the mere fact that we have lived.

It is what difference we have made to the lives of others

that will determine the significance of the life we lead.

Nelson Mandela

▼▼▼▼

Amram, you need to come home. We have some bad news. Please come home NOW.

The message could not have been clearer, but the timing was terrible. Amram was at Westminster College working toward his master's degree, and it was the week of midterm exams. Surely, Noelle wouldn't have contacted him if it hadn't been urgent. She understood the stress he was under with an incredibly tight schedule of school, work, and choir responsibilities.

Amram packed up his books and ran to the bus stop, praying he wouldn't have to wait long. As the city bus rounded the corner and made its way up the street in front of the school, Amram felt a small moment of relief. After boarding the bus and finding a seat, that relief was quickly replaced by apprehension. Noelle wouldn't talk about the news over the phone, and Amram didn't argue. Her voice was solemn as she assured him that they would talk when he returned home.

Is something wrong with Noelle? Maybe my family in Kenya?

Thoughts swirled as Amram considered the possibilities. As the bus slowly came to a deliberate stop a block from Amram's home, his patience was tested as he stood and waited for the doors to open. Immediately after they parted, he skipped a step and bounded out the doors toward home. Once inside the front door, he saw Noelle standing by the front window. She had obviously been watching for him.

"Amram, I don't know how to say this."

"What is happening? Just tell me," Amram insisted.

"I heard from your family, and there's been some terrible news. It's your dad." Noelle's voice trembled and her eyes filled with tears. "He . . . he died this morning."

"What? I just talked to him last night on the phone. Are you sure?"

Amram's emotions were firing in every direction, and he tried to sort through them so he could focus, but the unexpected lunacy of it all fought against the reality of what he was hearing. It just didn't make sense.

"I'm sorry, Amram. I'm so sorry," Noelle whispered.

Amram felt his knees buckle and grabbed the back of the chair to steady himself.

I just heard his voice last night. We prayed together . . . Oh, dear Lord, not my dad.

The two had talked about Amram's accomplishments and all the great things that were happening for him during this time of sacrifice and hard work. It had been two years since Amram's marriage, and in 2008 life was moving forward on schedule. Then the conversation turned to his father. He had been busy in his church work in the village and wasn't feeling well lately, so they had prayed together on the phone asking God for strength to endure each of their journeys. The conversation had been uplifting and tender.

Amram's head fell, and his shoulders began to shake as great sobs came from the depths of his soul. Noelle wrapped him in her arms as Amram's raw emotion spilled and disbelief caught up with the devastating reality. Amram found his voice and wept through what felt like unfairness and injustice.

"He wanted to come here and see me," Amram sobbed. "It's been so long . . . ten years since we've seen each other."

. . .

"I need to fly to Kenya immediately. My father has passed away, and I'll have to miss a few choir practices."

Even in his haste to secure an airline ticket and contact his school professors, Amram had remembered to contact the Tabernacle Choir president and alert him to the sudden plans. Because of the last-minute airline cost, Noelle would stay at home in Salt Lake so they could afford the exorbitant ticket price for Amram.

"Don't worry about the practices, Amram. I'm sorry about your father." The air between the two on the phone call was heavy with the somber news. It was clear that Amram was suffering.

The choir leadership had seen Amram's resilience and incredible dedication to everything in his life. Amram's ability to focus and tackle difficult paths had impressed all who knew him, but this was going to be tough. Everyone understood that his father was a musician and had influenced Amram's own love for music.

"Amram, I'll keep you in my prayers. Go take care of your family in Kenya, and we'll catch you up when you return. Remember to wear your name tag when you travel. You are a missionary, Amram. You have that mantle and all the blessings that come with it as a member of the choir. You will be carried."

. . .

Eyes often looked up at Amram's face, then down to the missionary badge on his shirt and back up with a questioning look. It was a conversation starter—people either knew of the Tabernacle Choir or asked Amram about it. He had attempted to answer questions and have a short discussion with other passengers in the airport about his involvement, but now that Amram was buckled into his assigned seat on the plane, he just wanted to be alone in his thoughts.

Amram closed his eyes in silent prayer. He prayed for safe travel and for the opportunity it provided to quickly get him to

Kenya. Amram felt a pang of gratitude for his membership in The Church of Jesus Christ of Latter-day Saints as his mind wandered in an attempt to understand his father's death. He knew that contrary to the way things were in Kenya, there was no fighting for leadership in the Church. People achieving leadership positions in many church denominations in Kenya were attacked if a group became jealous of perceived success or angry due to any theological or procedural differences. Sudden deaths due to poisoning were not uncommon.

Amram's father had reached a high point in his church responsibilities of ministering to the sick and dying. Because of his strong faith, he was often requested by families who were suffering or preparing the deceased for funerals. Amram's father embraced the esteemed opportunities to serve and love others in the village by praying for them and asking God to bless their lives. It was a heartfelt service for which he demanded nothing.

There were many who knew that Amram had achieved college degrees in America, something that was recognized as an extraordinary accomplishment. Some might have worried that he would return to Kenya and provide a better life for his father, something that would create opportunities in their eyes for his father's future success in the village and church leadership.

Amram's father had been tested at the hospital recently due to ongoing symptoms of illness, but nothing had been found. A thought suddenly stung Amram: *Could they have been slowly poisoning my dad?*

He was certain that poisoning was the cause of death, but there would never be proof. It was a question that would never be fully answered.

Amram knew of his father's deep wish to see him again, and the tragedy of the sudden death eradicating that dream seemed to dominate his emotions. In all Amram's previous battles and sufferings, he had prayed for miracles and trusted God would reveal a path, but this was different. Amram needed a miraculous balm of peace for his troubled soul.

. . .

Between the international flight and bus rides, it had been one long, exhausting day of travel. In the hours since he'd left Salt Lake City, Amram had barely eaten anything and had found it impossible to sleep. On his final bus ride in Kenya, Amram's hand rubbed his forehead, then dropped down to knead the back of his aching neck. The day had taken a toll, but despite a weary body and mind, Amram's first destination was sure— the morgue.

Amram walked in the front entrance; a kind woman greeted him then asked how she could help. It would be the first time since his father's death that Amram would say his father's name out loud. Amram noticed it felt wrong, strange, almost dream-like that he was here in Kenya after so many years and that he was declaring his father's name under these circumstances.

"Musungu," Amram said softly. "He's my father. I'm here to see his body."

The woman looked inside a file folder that lay on the desk where she was seated.

"Yes, follow me."

Amram was escorted down the hall into a room where a body lay on a table draped with a white cloth. The woman glanced up at Amram before placing her hands on the top edge of the fabric. His eyes signaled that he was ready, so she slowly pulled the cloth down to reveal a lifeless, gray face.

"Dad," Amram whispered as he choked back tears. "It's me, Am."

The woman took a step back to allow some space for the private moment.

"I'm back home. Right here with you, Dad."

Just the sight of his father filled Amram with an overwhelming sense of love and admiration for this kind man. Suddenly, his father's lips were almost moving as if he wanted to talk. It was only the slightest movement but was immediately noticed by Amram.

Does he want to tell me something?

Amram gently lay his hand on his father's, then watched in wonder as tears emerged from his father's eyes and slowly ran down his father's cheeks. It was a surreal moment where Amram felt deeply and powerfully connected to his father. A reunion of two souls united in some spiritual sphere where words were felt, not heard. Surely, this was a beautiful gift from God. Amram bowed his head in gratitude to know in his heart that he mattered to God. His father mattered. God knew they both needed this moment.

Amram looked up at the woman standing off to the side of his father's body.

"Did you see that?" he asked. The woman quietly nodded, her eyes wide.

"I won't be leaving his side for a while," Amram stated. He pointed across the room to a chair in the corner. "I'll just pull that chair over here and sit with him."

The mourning period in Kenya is traditionally three days before the deceased are returned to their village for burial. Amram continued to sit by his father's side throughout that time, rarely sleeping and taking only small breaks for food. The dedicated time allowed Amram to not only ponder his own upbringing and all the sacrifice his father had made in his behalf, but how he might honor that gift in return. Certainly, he would complete his father's temple work in the future, continue to care for and watch over his beloved mother, and assume his father's strong role in the family of maintaining and nurturing strong family relationships. Amram silently promised his father that he would strive every day to make him proud.

. . .

Before the burial, Amram went to the village to dedicate his father's grave. Others noticed the reverence Amram felt toward the sacred act of using his priesthood. There were tender conversations with others surrounding the priesthood and fullness of the gospel, and Amram embraced the opportunity to teach about God's beautiful plan. Extended family members and friends could feel the power of Amram's testimony.

Because of his faith and understanding of the gospel, Amram knew his family would be together again. He wondered if his older sister, grandmother, and other deceased family members were gathered with his father now. Surely, there was rejoicing in heaven, and Amram felt a sense of peace envisioning the homecoming. He would use that peace and comfort to move forward in forgiveness and love.

Before returning home to his wife in Utah, Amram gently spoke to his mother about embracing that comfort and peace. That conversation allowed his mother to share her own great faith.

"Mom, will you feel afraid living alone?" Amram asked. He wanted so much to calm all her worries.

"No, Am," she explained. "I am not afraid because I know with all my heart that God loves me and is watching over me."

It was a testament of the kind of faith and conviction that had seen her through many years and difficult circumstances. Amram's heart soared to hear his mother's strong faith and conviction spoken during such a raw and vulnerable time. In a moment when Amram intended to tenderly reach out and provide reassurance and peace for his mother, she had once again reached down into that beautiful heart of hers and taught him.

Amram and his mother.

· · ·

Amram felt the emotion rise in his chest, then felt a single tear roll down his cheek. He focused on the power of the words and continued to push forward through the music. The beautiful Tabernacle Choir voices all harmonized and came together to testify of eternal hope and assurance during their performance. Standing amid the choir was like participating in a surround-sound experience. Soon a second tear came, and then a third, but Amram continued to sing.

O my Father, thou that dwellest
In the high and glorious place,
When shall I regain thy presence
And again behold thy face?
In thy holy habitation,
Did my spirit once reside?
In my first primeval childhood
Was I nurtured near thy side?

When I leave this frail existence,
When I lay this mortal by,
Father, Mother, may I meet you
In your royal courts on high?
Then, at length, when I've completed
All you sent me forth to do,
With your mutual approbation
Let me come and dwell with you.

Never had Amram felt such a profound love and gratitude for both heavenly and earthly fathers in his life. How precious was the principle of eternal families! "O My Father" would continue to tug on Amram's heart, whether he was performing future concerts with the Tabernacle Choir or singing with his church congregation. It was a song of love. A hymn with enduring lyrics of peace.

It was a whisper of hope. . . .

KENYA

Figure 6
Women walking along a sand road.

CHAPTER ELEVEN

▲ ▲ ▲ ▲

Studying the gospel and sharing it daily can be

accomplished by anyone with or without an official call.

Please remember that it doesn't take a name tag to do missionary work!

M. Russell Ballard

▼ ▼ ▼ ▼

It was the downtrodden expression that caught Amram's attention. Dark eyes daring to make contact in the hope that someone might notice and offer some help. The homeless man was dirty and muttered a request for food.

"Sure, okay," the co-worker said. He waved a hand that signaled the homeless man to enter the small café.

Amram was out on a quick lunch break with other employees from work. It was an opportunity to grab a bite to eat and stretch their legs along the sidewalks of downtown Salt Lake City. The co-worker ordered his lunch at the counter, then turned and shot a condescending smile toward the homeless man.

"No, I'm not buying. I'm not spending money on *you*," the co-worker spat.

The others smirked at the meanspirited display and rushed up to the counter to order their own food. Amram's heart sank as he watched the homeless man step back. Who knew what circumstances in life had put this man on the street? Everyone had a story, and Amram understood that firsthand.

"Come here," Amram said to the homeless man, "I'll pay for your meal. Order whatever you'd like." Amram didn't have much, but he would order just a small drink for himself today in order to help.

The man looked over at Amram with soft eyes of gratitude. The order was placed, and the cashier looked up at Amram who nodded that he would pay the fifteen-dollar bill. Back at the table, Amram's co-workers shook their heads and snickered as he approached and pulled a chair out to take a seat.

"Amram, why would you spend your money on *those* people?" one said.

Amram looked at the others who stared wide-eyed at the situation, waiting for his response. Anger at their behavior was pushed aside and words were carefully chosen.

"Put yourself in that situation for a moment," Amram said. "What if it was *you* asking for help." Nobody said a word, so Amram continued. "Sometimes we can do good things, little things here and there, and with even humble means we can bless others. If you're rich, that's a good thing, because you have resources to bless and transform, but if not, you can still do your best to reach out. It might not even be in terms of money, but in showing interest and trying to talk to them. Maybe finding out what's going on and finding services that can help them."

The group of men sat a little lower in their seats. Heads were down, and no one was making eye contact with Amram.

"I know one thing for sure," Amram said. "The Lord puts people in our path who He knows we are able to help."

. . .

"Brother Musungu, this is Elder Oaks. I'd like to stop by your home for just a minute on my way to the temple to give you a small gift. Would that be okay?"

Elder Dallin H. Oaks was a member of the Quorum of the Twelve Apostles. He and Amram had exchanged some words in the past as their paths crossed at various church conferences. Amram was surprised to hear the Apostle's voice on the phone.

"Sure," Amram replied. "I'll be there and would love to see you."

Early the following morning, Amram heard a quiet knock at the door. He opened it to see Elder Oaks standing at the threshold.

"Hello, Brother Musungu. It's early in the morning, and I have only a minute. Sister Oaks is waiting in the car."

Amram and his wife had been invited to dinner in Elder Oaks's home, but the Apostle had never been here to Amram's apartment. It was simple but provided a modest place for two newlyweds.

"I'm so proud of all the missionary efforts you've been engaged in over the past several years, Brother Musungu," Elder Oaks said, "and I also appreciate your dedication to the choir."

"Thank you," Amram replied. "My greatest joy is sharing the gospel in any way that I can. We have continued to gather Israel as our dear prophet, President Gordon B. Hinkley, has admonished members of the Church throughout the world."

Elder Oaks had been holding a book in his hands. Now, he held it out in front of him and smiled.

"This is my book, and I wanted you to have a signed copy," Elder Oaks said. "Jesus taught the lessons in this book to the people in both word and example. The title, *The Lord's Way*, is exactly that—His way of living. You are a great example of that, and I thought you might enjoy the book."

"Wow, I appreciate that, and I will start reading it today!" Amram exclaimed. What kindness. Amram was touched that he would make such a personal visit. He couldn't wait to learn what this inspired Apostle had to say in his book.

Amram poured over the book for the next several days. It contrasted the way of the Lord and compared it to the ways and methods of the world. Amram particularly loved the section on caring for the poor and needy. He had been on the receiving end of this so many times, and he had promised Heavenly Father in his heart that he would always pay it forward. Amram knew in his heart that serving others who were less fortunate wasn't just the right thing to do, but something that brought him great joy. Amram thanked Heavenly Father for great leaders who continued to teach and inspire the world to be stronger disciples of Christ.

"Jambo!" Amram shouted.

He and Noelle were driving home from an evening in downtown Salt Lake City and noticed a couple with five children walking along the side of the road. He didn't know if they were from Africa, but the impression to stop was sure, and the Swahili greeting meaning "hello" came out of his mouth as he rolled down his window and pulled over beside them.

Fabian and Rosette Bahati and their five surprised children turned toward the voice. They didn't speak any English, but Swahili was somewhat familiar. A brief exchange indicated they had just arrived days before from the Democratic Republic of Congo as refugees of the war-torn country in central Africa.

As Amram spoke Swahili and Noelle spoke French, they were able to communicate. Amram and Noelle asked the couple where they lived and learned it was an apartment close to theirs. The family piled into the back seat of the Musungu car, and together they drove to the Bahati apartment.

Once inside, Amram and Noelle learned the Bahatis had no money and only one gallon of milk in the refrigerator. The children were scheduled to start school in a few days. Amram's eyes met Noelle's, and with a nod of the head there was mutual understanding. The few hundred dollars in their savings account would serve this family.

"Come with us, and we'll take you to the grocery store

tonight. We have some money to pay for some food for your family and school supplies for the children."

Tears filled the eyes of the Bahati family as two parents explained to the children that they would have food. Amram and Noelle walked the aisles of the store with Fabian and Rosette, explaining which foods were similar to those in Africa. Then they focused their attention on the children and helped them find a few items necessary to get started in school. After returning to the apartment, Noelle taught Rosette how to use the stove in the apartment.

The next day, Amram and Noelle returned to the Bahati apartment to check on the family and offer guidance that would help them further understand living in the United States. After spending more time answering questions, Amram and Noelle stood to leave. Fabian shook his head and looked over at his wife then back at their new friends.

"We have never met anybody who cared so much about us," Fabian asked. "I mean . . . we just met you. Maybe you are different, and we want to know why you are this way? Why have you done so much good for us?"

"We live our beliefs in Jesus Christ and try to follow His example," Amram answered. "We can get missionaries to teach you about those beliefs, and you're welcome to come to church with us. We'll drive you there, and Noelle and I will be there to translate for you."

Soon the Bahati family was baptized, and other extended family members followed. One year later, Amram and Noelle sat in the Salt Lake Temple and witnessed Fabian and Rosette being sealed for eternity by Elder Neil L. Anderson of the Quorum of the Twelve. He was fluent in French and able to perform the ordinance in the Bountiful Utah Temple.

Ultimately, the family stayed strong in the gospel, and many attended various universities to pursue their education. It continues to be a testament to Amram and Noelle of miracles through simple means. All the blessings and tender mercies for this family started with a quiet prompting and just one word.

Jambo.

. . .

Amram looked down at his feet and considered they had carried him for miles and miles his entire life. In those early years, his bare feet ran to school for miles through the African brush, and later they carried him for miles throughout Kenya and Tanzania as a missionary searching for those ready to hear the gospel. Today his feet would run a different kind of race.

The sun hadn't peeked above the horizon yet, but Amram was awake and eager to arrive at the starting line with the other racers. He tied the laces and said a quick prayer of gratitude for feet that had carried him all over the world blessing his life. The *Deseret News* Marathon was going to be a great opportunity to meet other runners from Kenya. Men and women also came from South Africa, Japan, New Zealand, and other countries as well as throughout the

United States to run the tough, hilly course that had once been followed by sixty thousand Latter-day Saint pioneers into the Salt Lake Valley.

Amram quickly recognized two international runners from Kenya. Zach Nyambaso had a strong finishing record for both half and full marathons, and John Kariuki had set a new record winning the *Deseret News* 10K race the year before. They talked among themselves and agreed to meet at the finish line. Amram suggested they come to his apartment following the race for a delicious Kenyan meal.

For the first six miles, Amram kept a good lead in the marathon, but he began to have knee problems and pulled back his pace. As he had done so many times in his life, he pushed through the obstacle and managed to finish the race. There was celebration in the air around the finish line, and many of the racers congratulated each other on their efforts. Amram, Zach, and John found each other and eventually climbed into Amram's car to head for a festive meal at his apartment.

"How do you like Salt Lake City?" Amram asked. Both indicated they loved the terrain with its scenic mountains and said they had felt welcomed by the people. Both expressed the desire to stay in Utah, but neither had the financial means to find a place to stay.

"You can both stay with me right here in my apartment if you don't mind sleeping on the floor," Amram offered. "We can all train together, and you won't have to worry about a thing. Just stay for a few weeks longer."

The offer was accepted, and the three men became fast friends. They trained together and learned more about what eventually brought each of them from Kenya to Utah. As Amram told his own story, the two men became interested in attending church on Sunday to understand more about Amram's passion for his beliefs. Soon Zach and John met with the missionaries, and both were baptized. Amram's missionary heart had continued to beat as his feet raced to change people's lives through an understanding of the gospel that answered so many questions. Amram was grateful for the amazing opportunity to share both his love for running and his love for the Lord.

One step at a time.

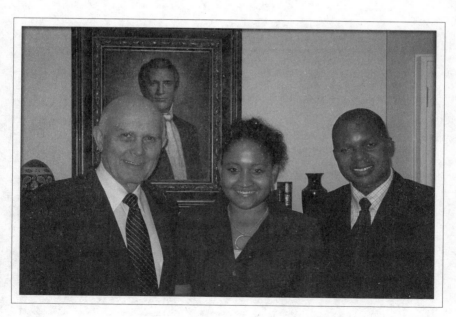

Elder Dallin H. Oaks in his home in Salt Lake City.
Amram and Noelle were invited to dinner.

Amram (center behind flag) and friends after marathon run in 2002.

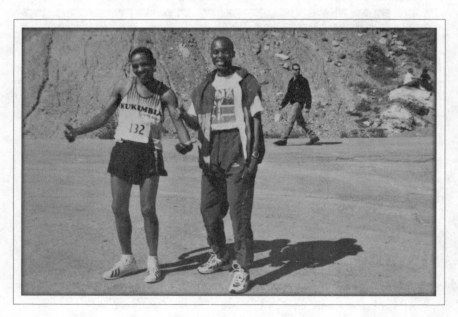

John Kariuki (international Kenyan runner) in Salt Lake City with Amram.

CHAPTER TWELVE

▲▲▲▲

Life is not a game of Solitaire. People depend on one another.

When one does well, others are lifted. When one stumbles, others also are impacted.

There are no one-man teams—either by definition or natural law.

Success is a cooperative effort; it's dependent upon those who stand beside you.

Jon Huntsman, Sr.

▼▼▼▼

Where is all the money going?

As an accountant and auditor, Amram understood budgeting and knew the importance of keeping a close watch on the outflows and inflows of finances. It was late in the evening, and Amram rubbed his eyes and focused on the bank statements and ledger. After a few minutes of review, the answer was clear—gasoline expenses were eating up a disproportionate part of their budget.

In 2008, gasoline prices were sky high and Amram's missionary travels were taking a toll on the family budget, but he and Noelle were still making ends meet. In addition, Amram and Noelle were expecting their first child. Amram and Noelle bowed their heads together in gratitude, thanking God for blessing them with enough to continue doing His work. Money was going to be tight with high gasoline prices, and personal time was entirely devoted to the cause, but it was all a sacrifice Amram was honored to endure. He was certain God would bless him as he juggled work, school, missionary opportunities, and obligations with the Tabernacle Choir. It was a full plate, but Amram knew that God was aware.

Amram's reputation as a strong missionary had spread throughout the Salt Lake Valley, and full-time missionaries were calling him on a regular basis to help teach people. Many were refugees from Africa and needed not only the lessons in Swahili but translation during church meetings. Investigators were attending English-speaking wards, and Amram's language skills were desperately needed to help them gain an understanding of gospel principles. Those wards were scattered far and wide in the Salt Lake Valley, which meant every Sunday and many weeknights Amram needed to drive his car to help in any way he could.

Noelle often attended the teaching appointments with Amram and was able to talk of her own conversion experience. Together they testified and taught how much the gospel had changed their lives and invited others to embrace their own faith and hope in Jesus Christ. Amram and Noelle loved meeting all the families, and their combined service brought great joy into their relationship.

Quickly, numbers began to multiply as interest in joining The Church of Jesus Christ of Latter-day Saints expanded. Full-time elders serving in the Salt Lake City area could hardly keep up with Amram's ambitious pace. Amram's phone never stopped ringing.

"Hello, President. I want to confirm that we have the building available for baptisms this Saturday," Amram said. He needed to confirm that all details were handled correctly, because this particular baptism was going to be a large event.

"Yes, Brother Musungu, it's all yours. How many baptisms this time?"

"We have twenty baptisms confirmed for this weekend. I'll be there to make sure everything goes smoothly," Amram promised.

"Did you say *twenty*?" the stake president asked. "Twenty baptisms on the same day?"

"Yes, President," Amram confirmed. He chuckled a bit before continuing. "The work is moving forward at an exciting pace, and I couldn't be happier about it. People are eager to be a part of this great gospel."

The explosion of missionary work a decade before in Kenya was happening again in the Salt Lake Valley, and both had one thing in common: Amram. Whether he was assisting other missionaries or striking up conversations in grocery stores and parks, Amram was sharing the reason for great joy in his life. Soon, the number of baptisms Amram played a direct part in through fellowshipping and teaching grew to more than three hundred.

In addition, Amram was serving as a stake missionary and anxiously engaged in the opportunity to encourage and persuade other members of the Church to share their testimony. He attended several classes and challenged members to share a copy of the Book of Mormon with their neighbors and friends at work. Amram promised to return weeks later to hear about the missionary experiences and motivate the members to continue their quest. Amram prayed his own enthusiasm for missionary work might be contagious.

. . .

"What am I seeing?" the doctor questioned.

Copies of the Book of Mormon were scattered over the section of highway he was approaching. Then he saw a car rolled over off the side of the road.

"Oh no! It must be missionaries!" *Who else would have this many copies of the Book of Mormon in their car?*

Amram saw the concerned face peering in the passenger window. Fortunately, the door wasn't damaged too badly, and Amram opened it carefully.

"I'm a doctor. Are you both okay?"

Amram looked over at his friend, who had been driving. It had been a trip together as friends to see the Manti Utah Temple and it was late in the evening. Maybe his friend had fallen asleep while driving. His friend nodded in confusion.

"I saw a bunch of copies of the Book of Mormon scattered over the road," the doctor said. "Are you missionaries?"

Amram smiled weakly. He was still trying to remember what had happened, but the question was funny to him.

"Yes, I'll always be a missionary," Amram replied. He always kept a box of about twenty books in the car so he would be prepared for every missionary opportunity. Amram never went anywhere without copies of the Book of Mormon and a hymnbook.

Fortunately, Amram escaped with minor bumps and bruises and not too much damage to the car. Amram was grateful for the protection and felt the Lord sent the doctor to care for them. Amram had been on the Lord's errand and recognized the watchful eye of His love and safekeeping. Later that evening, Amram held Noelle in his arms and expressed his thanks to the Lord for small miracles.

. . .

"Hello, my name is Amram Musungu, and I'm here to help you."

Eyes were wide, and faces displayed a combination of relief and shock. Amram understood the emotions they must be feeling, and that's why he was here. The refugee families had recently arrived in the United States through the help of various religious and governmental agencies, and they came from places like Burundi, Democratic Republic of Congo, Rwanda, and Southern Sudan to escape the civil strife. They were thankful to be safe but dismayed at the language and cultural differences in this new country.

Amram and Noelle volunteered countless hours with agencies like Angels in Action and American Red Cross to help provide resources and guidance to the flood of refugees looking for a better life. Families needed to learn basic tasks like using water faucets on showers and dials on washing machines. Many had lived for years in refugee camps enduring extreme poverty, and many didn't understand the refugees' prior living conditions, but Amram did. The joy and light Amram saw in their faces after serving the refugees was priceless.

Once the basics were learned, they moved on to more complicated things such as learning English, dealing with social situations, and finding a job. An eventual understanding of career goals, budgeting principles, and work ethics set the refugees up for success in the United States. It took time, but the commitment resulted in paths leading to bright futures.

The cultural differences between nations in Africa and the United States are also huge, and refugees needed to be taught everything from acceptable discipline and communication within the family to helping teens stay away from crime and gang activity. Amram has continued the efforts he began during those early years, making a significant impact in the lives of many.

Over the years, Amram has organized and coached champion African refugee soccer teams. The camaraderie and obligation to the team helps kids build a strong sense of self-esteem, physical fitness, and a belonging to something positive. Ultimately, Amram's devotion to the refugee soccer teams keeps the teens off the streets.

Amram often sees hundreds of people each week during his volunteer work. He loves organizing service projects that provide opportunities for both refugee participation and others who are looking for ways to help. Those refugee families who commit to the program and spend some time interacting with Amram eventually ask him about his religious beliefs and why he contributes so much selfless time. It is a question he is thrilled to answer.

Amram (top right) playing and coaching the refugee soccer team in 2009.

Amram also founded The HELM Foundation Inc., whose mission is to improve the lives of women and children in underdeveloped countries. His foundation plans to build a Hope Complex Center in Kenya to support this cause as well as to supply nutrition, clean water, and medical supplies for families. Educating and empowering women and children is a strong focus, as are networking with hospitals and drug companies to supply vaccinations for women and children.

Internationally, Amram gives presentations and manages both federal and private grants to provide education and training for the orphans and widows of HIV/AIDS. He is also active in the implementation of effective public health strategies to reduce the spread of this disease. Amram's voice is critical to this mission because of his English, Swahili, and other language skills, and his multilingual ability gives him the capacity to communicate with the target population and local and political leaders to support his foundation's efforts.

Receiving distinguished Ensign College Alumni Award from President Woodhouse in 2005.

Although Amram is proud of the sacrifice he's made to achieve multiple educational degrees and certifications, he is most honored by his work and devotion to lifting others through service. The Alumni Achievement Award, Utah Women Alliance Award, and the Graduate Class Distinguished Alumni Award recognized Amram's incredible dedication of scholastic excellency and countless hours serving the less fortunate. However, Amram's greatest joy often comes in the form of an email or a phone call from someone whose life Amram touched.

One of those phone calls began, "Amram, I got your number from someone at the agency. I hope you don't mind."

"Hello! How can I help you?" Amram responded. It seemed his cell phone never stopped ringing with the many who needed guidance.

"My name is Jamila, and I came here years ago as a poor refugee. I have a question to ask you."

"Sure," Amram answered.

"Do you know who baptized me?" Jamila asked.

"I would have to check the records, but I can certainly—"

"You," Jamila said, interrupting Amram. "You baptized me years ago, and I just needed to call and tell you that you changed my life."

"Oh, I appreciate that. I didn't recall the name," Amram stammered. *There have been so many; I can't keep track of all the names.*

"I just wanted to thank you and let you know that my life is good. I am married now to a very good man, and I am getting my master's degree at the University of Utah. It's all because of you, Amram. You helped me find happiness."

Amram's heart swelled with joy, and his eyes welled up with tears as he heard the emotion and gratitude in Jamila's voice. All he wanted to do was love the people and truly inspire them to rise up and become better. Every night he prayed that with the Lord's help, he might continue to make a difference in his own unique way. People like Jamila were a testament to Amram that his prayers were being answered.

One rescued soul at a time.

. . .

"Amram, you need to come soon. It's Richard . . . he's near the end."

"Oh, I'm so sorry, Marian. I will be right there," Amram said, hoping to console his friend. As soon as he saw her name pop up on his cell phone, he anticipated grim news. His heart broke as he considered what a difficult time this must be for Richard's wife, Marian, and the rest of the family.

Richard and Amram had a decades-long history together that started in the late nineties when Elder Richard P. Lindsay was sent to Kenya as an Area Authority for Africa to oversee Kenya's first district conference. Richard knew at the time that a tremendous amount of growth in that area was attributed to the missionary zeal of a boy named Amram Musungu. The two maintained a close friendship, and once Amram arrived in Utah, he became like family to Richard and his wife. How honored Amram and Noelle had been to have the Lindsays attend their temple wedding!

On numerous occasions, Richard chided Amram on his ambitious dreams and promised Amram that if he ever ran for political office in Utah, he hoped he would be around to become Amram's chief campaigner. Richard Lindsay had a great political career in the sixties and seventies as a Utah State Senator and member of the Utah House of Representatives. Over the years, the two maintained a strong friendship of mutual respect for service in the state of Utah and a shared love for the opportunity to do the Lord's work. However, Richard's time on earth was cut short by a cancer diagnosis, and the fight was nearly over.

Amram entered the hospice area feeling a great wave of sadness. This great man had touched so many lives, including Amram's life. Marian ushered him into the room then stepped over to Richard's bedside.

"Richard," she whispered, "Amram is here."

Amram took a place next to his great friend as Richard reached up and grabbed Amram's arm. Richard held Amram's arm tight with a strong grip for several minutes as tears rolled down both men's cheeks. They both recognized it as goodbye for now. Two men understood and knew they would see each other again in another spiritual realm. Heaven would soon receive a great servant of the Lord, but Amram still had more to accomplish, and Richard knew he wouldn't be on earth to see it. Richard would continue to cheer Amram on from above as Amram progressed and passionately moved forward building the kingdom of God. Richard closed his eyes, remembering the young, barefoot boy who had made such an impression on him long ago.

There goes the future of the Church.

KENYA

Figure 7
Lake Nakuru lying in the Great Rift Valley.

CHAPTER THIRTEEN

▲▲▲

Our Heavenly Father expects the best from each of us.

We must believe in ourselves. Don't give in when the going gets rough.

You are laying the foundation of a great work,

and that great work is your life.

Jon Huntsman Sr.

▼▼▼

Amram took a deep breath and smiled. He had never seen this coming but knew the Lord's hand was involved. He marveled at the opportunity to be the Swahili voice for the world. Amram imagined families in Kenya gathered together to hear the April 1999 general conference addresses and was honored to be the voice to deliver the messages.

Amram adjusted the headset and looked on the table in front of him at the translated copy of the first speaker's address. He would have to listen to the address in English and speak the Swahili words in sync with the speaker. Amram felt prepared but knew the speakers often strayed from their prepared words when they felt inspired to do so, and he knew he would have to be ready to make that immediate modification. It was an immense responsibility to translate the words of the prophet and other great leaders of The Church of Jesus Christ of Latter-day Saints and to ensure that his translation would be accurate. Amram had pleaded with the Lord for help, and he believed assistance from the heavens would carry him through this great calling.

When the Church's language director told Amram that the Church wanted to add the Swahili language to the list of available general conference translations and wanted him to pioneer that effort, Amram was overcome with joy. It was another facet of missionary work that enabled him to be directly involved in teaching the gospel. Over the next ten years, Amram would teach the gospel through his translated words of the prophet and other Apostles at general conference, but this first time felt meaningful.

Amram reflected on the first time he heard a general conference address so long ago in the small Kibera Branch in Kenya. At fourteen, Amram's understanding of the English language was not complete, but he had felt the spirit of the words. Now, so many in Africa would be able to embrace a fuller understanding in their own Swahili language.

Amram spoke tender words in his heart seconds before the start of the conference. *Heavenly Father, I am honored be here and to deliver the love and spirit of these words to the great people of Africa.*

President Gordon B. Hinkley stood and eagerly walked up to the pulpit to open the April conference. "Welcome to conference! We again welcome you, my brothers and sisters, to this great world conference."

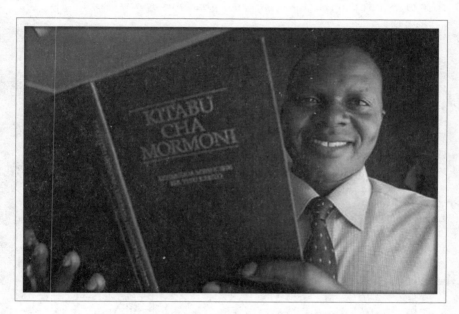

Amram felt a warm burning in his chest as he leaned into the microphone and began to speak the prophet's words in Swahili.

"Karibuni kwenye mkutano! Tunawakaribisha tena, ndugu na dada zangu, katika mkutano huu mkubwa wa ulimwengu."

Amram holding the Book of Mormon translated into Swahili.

Amram stood and faced the team members with whom he had worked countless hours for the past three years translating the Book of Mormon, Doctrine and Covenants, Pearl of Great Price, *Gospel Principles*, and *Joseph Smith Testimony* pamphlet into Swahili. He was proud to have been asked to participate in such a momentous undertaking, and he now joined a gathering in the Church Office

Building to celebrate the completion of their work. Those in charge had asked Amram to say a few words.

"I know there are people in Kenya, Tanzania, Burundi, and Congo who need to read these sacred words in Swahili," Amram began. "The work we have done here will touch the lives of people we will never meet in person, but I can testify this work will change them and bless their lives. We have all been part of a great missionary work."

Amram's eyes filled with tears as he continued. "When I served my full-time mission in Kenya and Tanzania as a young man, I longed to have a Swahili Book of Mormon for investigators. Because of our efforts, missionaries will now be able to provide these for the people so they can feel these words and fully learn the gospel."

Amram felt joy in his heart as his eyes scanned all who had sacrificed for the work.

"I'm honored to have been a part of this work with you and other team members in Kenya who assisted us with this huge project. What a blessing this has been in my life to serve the Lord and His beloved people in Africa."

. . .

Fabian and Rosette Bahati took their seats in the Bountiful Utah Temple, placed the headsets on top of their heads, and adjusted the earphones. They were one of the first members to benefit from the temple session that had been previously recorded and translated into Swahili. Emotions were tender as Amram recalled his first encounter with this family along the side of a road in Salt Lake City. Now he was here to witness Fabian and Rosette continue their devoted journey in the Church. The Swahili translation of temple ordinances had been finished just in time for Amram to witness the sacred event. It was a full-circle moment that began with the simple greeting, *Jambo*.

Three years earlier, Amram had overseen a team of Church members in Kenya who were given part of the responsibility to work on the ordinance translations. Recently, the Church had flown the team to the Salt Lake Temple to make the official recording. Amram was trusted to oversee the recording and ensure that every spoken word was perfectly enunciated and accurate. It had been a long, twelve-hour workday with the Kenyan team to achieve a perfect and flawless Swahili recording.

What a blessing this would be for Swahili-speaking members of the Church worldwide. Amram was humbled that the Lord had continued to direct Amram on paths toward more missionary work in a variety of ways. Every day Amram knelt in prayer and asked for new opportunities to serve, and those prayers continued to be answered over and over. It was exciting, exhausting, and humbling.

Amram and Noelle embraced the Bahatis after the temple session and felt the significance of their paths crossing in the past years. Tears of joy were shed, and smiles revealed a love for each other and a shared testimony of the Lord. It was a moment recognized as a tender mercy sprouting from seeds of missionary work, friendship, and peace.

. . .

How will I do everything required of me? I'm going to need the Lord to give me strength to endure everything I am being asked to do. . . .

The thought persisted as Amram decided to look over his class notes one more time. He felt prepared for this new teaching experience, but the hour-long bus ride from Salt Lake City to the campus of Brigham Young University in Provo allowed time for one final glance through his outline.

Amram's mind flashed back to years of running through the brush to attend school in Kenya. How could he have foreseen a future of returning to the classroom? This, however, would be very different from that humble experience of a barefoot boy sitting under a tree in a small, cleared area dedicated to learning in elementary school. Today Amram would stand at the front of the college classroom in a very different role—that of Professor Musungu.

What a privilege it was to create a new Swahili language course for the curriculum at Brigham Young University. As the most widely spoken language approved by the African Union, Swahili is taught in more than sixty universities in the United States. Now with Amram's direction, BYU would be included in that group.

On paper, the commitment didn't make sense. Amram's obligations seemed greater than time could possibly allow. His teaching schedule for two evenings a week in Provo was a heavy time commitment in addition to his full-time accounting job, graduate school studies, Tabernacle Choir practices and performances, work with volunteer and refugee organizations, and his continuing missionary work in the Salt Lake area. Once again, Amram trusted that God was opening doors for him to serve, and he promised to do his best.

Professor Musungu watched as the students began to filter into the classroom. Eleven students would fill chairs that first semester, but the class popularity soon doubled the student numbers. Eventually, Professor Musungu created a two-year Swahili language program with more classes. It was his goal to teach the culture as well as the language. Once a week, he taught students how to cook Swahili food, and together they played Swahili games and sang Swahili songs. Occasionally he invited all his students to his home for an evening of Swahili food and family fun.

Many of the students went on to volunteer for service opportunities in Kenya and Tanzania with their new language skills. Some wanted to listen to general conference addresses in Swahili to test their understanding. One thing was certain: all of Professor Musungu's students felt a strong connection to him, and they would keep in touch with their mentor for years.

Amram would teach for ten years at Brigham Young University. Ten years of love, dedication, and a commitment to learning what always began with one word at the start of each semester.

Jambo.

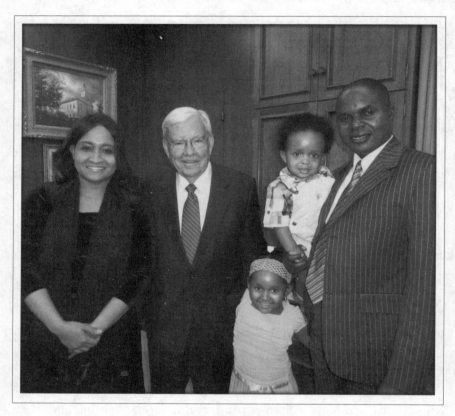

Elder M. Russell Ballard in his church office with Amram, Noelle, and their two children.

CHAPTER FOURTEEN

▲▲▲▲

Only a life lived for others is a life worthwhile.

Albert Einstein

▼▼▼▼

"Brother Musungu, this is Elder Evans in south Salt Lake City. I'm one of the full-time missionaries here, and I was told to call you."

"Sure, Elder Evans. How can I help you?" Amram replied. He was not surprised, as it was not uncommon to receive daily phone calls from any of the full-time missionaries serving in the vicinity of the Utah Salt Lake City Mission.

"My district leader says you are the one to call for a Swahili translation. We're teaching a family here who came over from Burundi, and they are eager to learn, but their English is minimal. My district leader tells me you are very busy . . ."

"Yes, Elder, but I'm always available for missionary work," Amram voiced.

"Well, we need your help with a missionary discussion, and I think this family wants to attend church with us on Sunday, but we'll need your Swahili language translations for both."

Amram paused for a moment as he considered his schedule.

It was becoming increasingly difficult to be in multiple meetinghouses and homes each week. Sundays were hardest of all, with many refugees and investigators attending English-speaking wards and understanding very little of what was said. To meet the need, Amram had to start early in the morning and drive to various buildings to attend meetings with the assorted families, translating everything that was spoken at the pulpit or by a teacher in class. Amram and Noelle were already sacrificing for the expense of the gasoline involved, but the time commitment was almost too much.

"Elder, let me know your availability, and I'll see what I can do. We'll make this work," Amram confirmed.

Amram was positive in his assurance as much for the missionary as he was for himself. Amram *wanted* to be of service, but the battle was *time*. There were needed Swahili translations for church meetings with both investigating and new members. Bishops often met with refugee families and called Amram to attend those discussions to learn what a family's needs were and how his congregation might be involved in service. Full-time missionaries throughout the region were calling on Amram every day to bridge a language barrier for teaching purposes. When Amram volunteered at refugee rescue centers, those friendships often developed and later turned into missionary opportunities where translation and guidance were needed as refugees requested to attend his church and learn more.

Amram was certain of one thing. Salt Lake City needed its own Swahili branch.

"These people need to come together and learn the gospel in their own language. If they understand the principles of self-reliance, serving others, and the doctrine of Jesus Christ, it will help them rise up and become better. I believe it will make a real difference in their lives."

"You don't have to convince me," President Ryan Olsen stated. "I've seen the time and work you've been putting into this effort, Brother Musungu." He also knew that Utah Salt Lake City Mission President William Blake Sonne concurred."

"We now have the scriptures translated into Swahili as well as the temple ordinances and even the general conference addresses. It is natural for a branch to be formed and utilize all that our Swahili translating teams have completed over the years," Amram explained.

President Olsen nodded in agreement. Surely, the Lord's hand was involved in this timeline of events, and He had certainly inspired Amram to move it forward.

"I've been working on statistics," Amram said as he pointed at figures on a spreadsheet. "These are numbers of families and those who I believe are ready to hold leadership positions in a Swahili branch, as well as other members who would be in a good position to help out. There are also some returned missionaries in the Salt Lake City area who served in Africa, and I've listed them here as well. They could be a great resource to get this branch started and running smoothly."

"That's great, Amram. Let's put it all together in an application to submit to Church headquarters. I think it would benefit our stake to host such a branch. It would give many of our members in the stake a great opportunity to serve."

The stake president smiled at Amram. President Olsen was eager to make it work with Amram. What ambition this young man had!

. . .

Amram sat up straight in the chair across the desk of President Olsen, hoping for good news. He believed with his whole heart and soul that the paperwork had been enough to fully inform those at Church headquarters of the need for a Swahili branch. He felt eager to hear the word *approved* and noticed his heart beating in anticipation.

"Brother Musungu, I'm delighted to tell you the branch has been approved," President Olsen declared.

An indescribable joy swept over Amram as he envisioned the gathering of so many who needed the Swahili language in learning and committing to the gospel. This was a miracle, and Amram felt proud to have initiated the proposal by baptizing hundreds who would now be attending this new branch. He felt speechless as he sat quietly, immersed in his own thoughts.

"Brother Musungu, what do you think about this?" President Olsen asked.

"This is such great news for the people. I feel such joy and gratitude. I'll certainly support the decision and help in finding leadership for the branch."

"Well, Brother Musungu, we cannot start a Swahili branch without you. I'd like you to be the branch president."

"I think I cannot have two callings, President Olsen. As you know, I am already singing in the Tabernacle Choir." Amram's mind began to swirl with the lists of responsibilities for all of his commitments—teaching at BYU, graduate school, full-time work, volunteer leadership, missionary work. . . . Amram's shoulders slumped forward slightly with the emotional weight of it all.

"I'll contact the choir leadership and let them know we're going to make an exception so you can do both," President Olsen assured.

Both? How can I do this? Amram's emotions were spinning.

Amram's thoughts shifted from doubt to a remembrance of the book Elder Dallin H. Oaks had given him not long ago—*The Lord's Way*. It was a book about committing your life to caring for the poor, the widows, the sick, and all others who might have different needs. Amram knew in that moment that Elder Oaks had been inspired to give him that book. Amram would need to partner with the Lord and trust that this path was right and that everything had led to this assignment.

"Okay," Amram said softly, "I will go where the Lord wants me to go."

Amram didn't know how this could work, but he knew from

so many experiences in his own life that nothing was impossible with the Lord. He would show up, work hard, and pray that the Lord would walk beside him on this journey and bless the other important things and people in his life. Amram felt a warm burning in his chest as a witness that this was exactly where he should be. He recognized the feeling and looked back up at President Olsen. Amram put his shoulders back and steadied his voice with the confidence only the Spirit could provide.

"I will do my best."

. . .

President Amram Musungu turned his beautiful, tiny daughter in his hands to look at her sweet face, then held her up high for the congregation to see. There were audible sounds of celebration as members of the Swahili Branch felt the importance of this moment. Amram's daughter was the first baby to be blessed in this new branch—blessed in Swahili and given the name of Mira Jane Musungu. Her middle name, Jane, was Amram's mother's first name.

The branch members were struggling to become one in purpose, and Amram hoped the baby blessing would be a sign of unity for the new branch. He prayed for them to come together as members of the Church and to love each other as God loves. To find harmony and joy in serving and worshipping together.

Such unity was not a simple thing to accomplish. Africa is

known for its tribalism, and many tribes don't get along together because of cultural and political differences. Those divisions were cropping up now in Salt Lake City as various groups of refugees gathered under one roof as members of the Swahili Branch.

"We cannot allow what divided us in Africa to divide us in the Church," President Musungu said. His voice was direct and serious as he spoke to the congregation from the pulpit.

"We have Hutu and Tutsi divisions in Africa that tear people apart. We cannot bring that here, my friends." Amram made eye contact with members of his congregation before continuing.

"I think we know that as members of the Church, we need to learn how to work together and help each other. We can do this if we change our hearts. We must live together as a family."

Tribalism was just one of many challenges faced by the branch. Transportation to the Swahili Branch was an issue for some families. Calls were made to couples in the Salt Lake region to provide the transportation for Swahili Branch members living in their neighborhoods. English-speaking classes were set up for those who could not speak the language; while those in the branch spoke Swahili, which eliminated the need for translation, Amram knew that branch members would never find a job if they couldn't speak the English language. Financial hardships were also rampant among branch members, and the leadership in the Swahili Branch reached out to other wards in the stake to provide much-needed service.

In the village streets of Africa, adults reach out and discipline and care for other people's children. That presented a cultural difference in the United States that was creating problems with young people roaming streets and neighborhoods without supervision. It required Amram to spend some time with law enforcement and in courthouses helping lawyers and judges understand the cultural differences. He pled for legal leniency with families who were innocent because of the contrast. Amram suggested patience with them as he promised future training and education for those in trouble.

Amram met with parents and young women in his branch about cultural differences in the United States. In Africa, many young women married as teenagers, but Amram urged them to pursue all the opportunities available to them before marriage.

"These young women have a future in America," Amram promised the parents. "Let them go to school, and they'll make good decisions along the way."

. . .

"We are a team. We all depend on each other. Every evening you must be at practice."

In order to help keep the boys and younger men off the streets and away from the temptations of drinking, Amram formed a soccer team; he also helped coach and played as they competed against other teams in the community. Soon enough, any team scheduled to play against the Swahili team knew they were in for a battle.

"We are Africa United," Amram shouted.

"Africa United!" the team responded.

In addition to keeping the refugees off the streets, membership in Africa United gave them purpose as they trained together and began to win games and tournaments. When Amram's schedule allowed, he played on the field with team members comprised of the Swahili Branch and other refugees, something that created a strong bond outside the meetinghouse walls. They all began to trust Amram's love and dedication to them. Amram could see it was making a difference.

Many of the boys on the soccer team went on to be awarded scholarships and attend universities. Girls who took the advice to wait for marriage began to earn degrees and find successful careers. The new focus began to steer this new generation of refugees toward a brighter future.

. . .

This is incredible. The numbers just keep growing. . . .

President Ryan Olsen looked at the baptismal report for his stake. Once again, the Swahili Branch's baptismal numbers dominated the new membership in the mission. All the baptisms for the entire mission were in that region. One word came to mind. *Amram.*

Amram didn't just *talk* about missionary work; his *actions* matched his testimony. Now he was sharing that fiery testimony with the members of the Swahili Branch and encouraging them to be missionary-minded. As the small branch grew and developed, the people began to share Amram's vision of what the gospel could bring to everyone's life.

President Amram stood in front of his congregation to announce the upcoming good news.

"We have ten baptisms this next Saturday. I hope to see you all there so we can welcome these new members and learn how to serve and love them into our family."

Amram took his seat on the stand as the organist began to play the familiar hymn entitled "Because I Have Been Given Much."

Amram's heart was full as he considered all the Lord's blessings in his life. The love he felt for the Savior was tender, and that love motivated Amram to emulate the Savior and devote his life to Him. He simply wanted everyone else to feel that same love. It was what drove his missionary efforts. Amram's heart burned as he remembered earlier pivotal moments in his young life.

If only Elder Price and Elder Thomas could sit on the stand with me and see how their own missionary efforts with me led to the beautiful gathering of these people in the Swahili Branch.

Amram wiped tears as he whispered the last line of the hymn in silent prayer.

I'll show that love by word and deed; thus shall my thanks be thanks in deed.

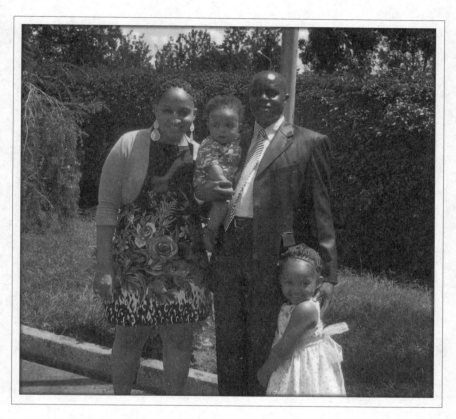

Amram, Noelle, Mira, and Wesley Musungu

Figure 8

Mount Kilimanjaro from Aboseli National Park.

▼▼▼

CHAPTER FIFTEEN

When words fail, music speaks.

Hans Christian Anderson

"Mr. and Mrs. Musungu, your son is very sick. The virus is affecting his heart, and we're going to transfer him to the Intensive Care Unit where we can watch him very closely."

The doctor's tone was serious. Amram looked over at Noelle and put his arm around her shoulders for support. How could this be? At only thirteen months old, their son was still so small. They had taken him to the hospital emergency room because they assumed he had the flu virus and his symptoms appeared to be getting worse.

Just more than a year earlier, the birth of a son completed the Musungu family. They chose the name Wesley Aaron Musungu, the middle name representing Amram's father's name. The biblical name of Aaron with a Hebrew meaning of *exalted and strong* felt right for their son. Amram and Noelle hoped this boy would carry the strength of his name and memory of his grandfather throughout his life to accomplish many great things. With their daughter, Mira Jane, and son, Wesley Aaron, life seemed to be perfect as Amram and Noelle pondered all the hopes and dreams for their beautiful children.

"Intensive Care Unit? The ICU?" Amram asked. He looked over at Noelle, whose chin was trembling. "I thought maybe you would keep him here for only a day or so. Is there no medicine that can help with the flu?"

"Whatever virus your son has is affecting his heart," the doctor explained. "We can run more tests and monitor his pulse and breathing with some very advanced machines in the ICU. He'll have his own nurse who will take good care of him."

"May we come with him?" Amram asked. He felt his reality slipping as he fought to stay focused. *How did this happen? I have so many questions.*

"Certainly. Your son is very weak, but he can still hear your voice. We want him to know that he is not alone." The doctor looked over at Noelle, who was now crying. "You can hold his hand and talk to him to provide comfort."

. . .

It had been a long, agonizing month watching little Wesley Aaron fight for his life in the ICU. Amram and his family knelt each morning to request strength for their child to battle the virus and for enlightened minds in the doctors and nurses who were caring for him. They also put his name on temple prayer rolls each week, knowing that if it was God's will that their son should live, all prayers both in homes and in holy temples would be answered.

Amram forced himself to show up at work each day as thoughts always wandered to the welfare of his son. It was difficult to be away from the hospital, but Amram knew he needed to financially support his family. His emotions felt fractured from the separation, but he found his way to the office every morning. Amram and Noelle shared and split the time they could devote to spending time with their very sick child in the hospital.

Amram would have to miss the next Tabernacle Choir tour. The director understood Amram's need to stay close and attend to his son. There would be more tours in the future, but the priority this time was family.

After weeks of fighting, the stress on Wesley Aaron's heart was so extreme that they hooked him up to a machine to provide life support. The extracorporeal membrane oxygenation (ECMO) was pumping Wesley Aaron's blood outside his body to a heart-lung machine that removed carbon dioxide from the blood. The machine then sent oxygen-filled blood back to tissues in his body. As the blood flowed from the right side of his heart to the membrane oxygenator in the heart-lung machine, it was rewarmed and sent back to his body. The method was allowing his blood to "bypass" the heart and lungs, allowing his organs to rest and heal.

Amram glanced at the clock and finished the transactions he had been working on at his desk. It was 9:30 in the morning. He pushed himself back from his computer, stood up, and slowly walked down the hallway to an empty conference room. It was the usual place for gatherings and workplace meetings, but since Wesley Aaron had been hospitalized, it became a daily place of refuge—a holy place for Amram every morning at 9:30.

Amram entered the conference room, locked the door behind him, and turned out the lights. He walked across the darkened room to a small clearing next to the large wooden table and fell to his knees. Amram took a deep breath and bowed his head in reverence before speaking.

"Dear Heavenly Father. . . ."

Heart-felt words spilled from Amram's soul as he asked for his son to be watched over and blessed. Amram uttered tender words of gratitude for the medical staff as he envisioned them providing compassion and assistance. He pled for mercy and miracles as he imagined the Lord's powerful hands directing this difficult course of his family's life. Amram had seen the Lord's hands so many times in his life and never doubted He was also very aware of Wesley Aaron.

Amram concluded his prayer, then pulled a chair over so he could sit down before calling the hospital. Every day he received a report from the medical staff by phone confirming that Wesley Aaron was still fighting. He felt enormous gratitude for the positive updates and committed to continue communicating with his Heavenly Father in the quiet conference room every morning before making the phone call.

The entire ICU staff grew to love the Musungu family and

were inspired by the family's conviction to their faith. Amram and Noelle visited as often as they could and had prayed vocally over their son on a regular basis over the past month. Occasionally, Amram and Noelle brought Mira Jane to the ICU to hold her little brother's hand and talk to him. The staff witnessed many moments of a little girl praying over her brother with a beautiful, child-like belief that God heard her prayers. Clearly this child had learned from parents that God not only heard prayers but loved her and was very aware of her little brother. It was a vision of humility and tenderness for all the medical workers.

. . .

"Mr. Musungu, we are having trouble with your son's blood pressure today," Dr. Sands reported. "We have given him all the drugs and done everything we can, but he is not responding as we had hoped. His blood pressure is way too high."

Amram gripped the phone tightly as he tried to gather his thoughts.

"You've tried everything?" Amram asked. It was a desperate question with an obvious answer.

"Yes, but we will continue doing what we can. I just wanted you to know the change in his condition, Mr. Musungu."

What can we do? There must be something. Amram's heart sank, and he silently pleaded for divine insight to help his little boy.

Suddenly, Amram had a strong thought.

Play music for him.

It was a quiet prompting, but one with certainty. *Music?* The Tabernacle Choir had recorded a CD of Primary children's songs, and the Musungu family played it often in their home as the children loved singing along to the music. The recording had been made while Amram sang with the choir.

Play the music for him.

The thought came again and was quiet, but sure.

"Dr. Sands, do you have a CD player there at the hospital that I can borrow? I want to play something for my son."

"Yes, we have one," Dr. Sands responded. It was an unexpected request and a rather abrupt change of subject. The doctor wondered where this was going.

"I'll be right there," Amram replied.

Amram ended the phone call and grabbed the Tabernacle Choir's recording of Primary children's songs. He wondered how this could help his critically ill son but didn't question the prompting. He ran into the other room to find Noelle and Mira Jane.

"Come quickly," Amram said. "Wesley is in trouble. His blood pressure is too high. We all need to go to the hospital now."

. . .

The nurse looked up to see Amram's concerned expression through the glass window of the ICU unit. The doctor had requested that the staff find a CD player for Mr. Musungu and explained that he was on his way to the hospital. The nurse waved at Amram and walked over to greet the family at the entrance. She understood their son was in a dangerous position. His little body was so tired of the weeks-long fight to live.

After greeting Amram and Noelle, the nurse looked down to see Mira Jane's wide eyes and smiled at the little girl.

"I see you've brought the whole family again."

The nurse looked up at Amram. "We have the CD player over by your son's bed. The doctor is here checking on him."

Amram thanked the nurse and swiftly walked over to stand next to his son. He opened the CD case and placed the recording in the player. Amram looked up to see the entire staff watching him. Nobody dared to move or speak.

Amram looked back down at his son. His little chest was heaving up and down; the simple act of breathing looked difficult.

"I brought something for you, Wesley," he said.

Noelle and Mira Jane inched closer to stand next to the bed. The doctor took a step back and watched Wesley's vitals on the machine.

Amram pushed the play button on the CD player, and his own voice along with the voices of the Tabernacle Choir began to fill the room with beautiful music and tender lyrics. Mira Jane smiled as she recognized the favorite song entitled "I Know That My Savior Loves Me." Words of love and hope filled the room. Noelle wiped a tear that slowly fell down her cheek.

Immediately Wesley Aaron's blood pressure dropped, and the numbers on the machine fell, reflecting the miraculous decline. Everyone in the room looked up at each other to confirm what they had just witnessed. As the Tabernacle Choir continued to sing, the doctor and nurses watched as the boy's numbers stayed low and his vital signs improved. The doctor shook his head as he witnessed Wesley Aaron's unexplained reaction. It was a moment in his career that medical science could not explain.

Amram began to weep.

Thank you, Lord, for this miracle.

The heavens had been opened. Amram turned to his family and the medical staff in the room. All eyes were moist.

"You are seeing Heavenly Father do His work right now," Amram said through tears. "The prescription our boy needed today was music."

. . .

It had been almost two months, but Wesley Aaron had continued to improve to the point that he could be released from the hospital. Amram and Noelle brought a small memory booklet to the medical staff so they could write their experiences and impressions in the keepsake. All the doctors and nurses had been touched by what they had seen and felt during their time with the Musungu family, and they all wrote heart-felt messages of hope and love for Wesley Aaron and experiences that testified of miracles.

Amram and Noelle would be sure to read the messages in the memory book to Wesley Aaron when he was older. It was a witness that small miracles can bring forth great blessings. And it was a beautiful testament of prayers being heard, even in the darkest moments of our life.

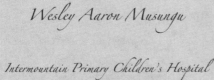

Wesley Aaron Musungu

Intermountain Primary Children's Hospital
Salt Lake City, Utah
2013

Lifetime Memories from my favorite treatment team

Thank you for making me feel better!

Wesley -
You have such a sweet family! It was a pleasure taking care of such a sweet boy! I'm glad that you are doing so well! Keep up the good work!
♡ LeRoyne RN
night nurse

Wesley,
We are starting to see your feisty side come out - and we like it! You are such a sweet and strong little guy & you couldn't be any cuter! I am happy to be taking care of you & can't wait to see & hear of the amazing things you do!
- Megan VanWagenen
PICU RN

Wesley -
It was a miracle to see you heal & to see the faith & hope your family had in you & in the medical staff who took care of you. I am grateful to have been a part of your care and to witness the miracle of your life. God Bless.
- Jorgan Jacobson
(PICU Tec
You Will Do Amazing Things!

WESLEY,
You are an amazing little boy. It is so fun to see the progress you are making everyday. You are very blessed to have such a wonderful family. May you have a long & wonderful life! ♡ Brookelyn
PICU RN

Page from the ICU Memory Book

164

Amram with his family. Happy and healthy.

KENYA

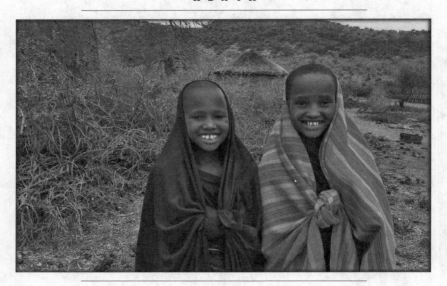

Figure 9
Maasai boys.

CHAPTER SIXTEEN

Never worry about numbers.

Help one person at a time and always

start with the person nearest you.

Mother Teresa

"Hey, Amram. I have something I think you'll be interested in."

"Larry Barkdull!" Amram replied. "Good to see you, my friend."

Larry was a kind, generous individual who possessed a strong missionary heart. He was the president of a social media site called Gospel Ideals International, and he volunteered countless hours spreading the good news of the gospel all over the world. The site was enlightening, informative, and served as an open invitation for anyone to ask questions about The Church of Jesus Christ of Latter-day Saints.

"I received a message on the Gospel Ideals site from someone in Africa who is inquiring about the Church," Larry said with a grin.

Amram's eyes lit up. Larry could see he had Amram's full attention.

"Would you like to talk to him?" Larry asked.

"Wow, you bet," Amram replied. "Do you know anything about him?"

"Yes. His name is Dr. Weston Kapasule, and he is a doctor of theology in Malawi. Another professor in a conference shared something about Latter-day Saints, and Dr. Weston found our site on social media and has reached out to learn more. He seems curious and eager."

"I'm on it," Amram smiled.

. . .

"Thank you for seeing me President Gillette," Amram said.

It was a cool day in 2012, and the crisp autumn air buoyed Amram's spirits and added vigor to his steps as he hurried across the Salt Lake Temple grounds to meet with Utah Salt Lake City Mission President David L. Gillette. The beauty of the temple against the orange, red, and yellow leaves was not unnoticed by Amram. He often marveled at the Lord's creations on earth and the visual majesty of it all.

"I have discovered a great missionary opportunity that I hope you can help me with," Amram said.

"Sure, how can I help?" President Gillette asked. He noticed Amram sitting on the edge of his seat keen to tell his story. He was always thrilled to see members excited about missionary service.

"I have been emailing back and forth with a Dr. Weston Kapasule in Malawi, Africa, who has an interest in the missionary discussions. He lives in the city of Kasungu, which is more than two hours away from the nearest branch, and there are no missionaries currently serving in Malawi. The Temple Square missionaries are called to teach people from anywhere in the world who come to visit, and. . . ."

Amram paused to allow President Gillette to catch up to Amram's excitement and to deliver the final pitch.

". . . I'd like to work with some missionaries here in your mission to teach Dr. Weston through phone calls. They don't have internet there, so we'll have to rely on teaching with the speaker on during the phone conversations."

Amram assumed this was an unusual request, but he was desperate to make it work. If there wasn't a mission in Malawi, he would bring the mission to them.

"I'll come here every week for as long as it takes and teach with whoever you select. I'm committed to making this work, and I am sure it will be a great missionary opportunity for your elders or sisters to teach with me."

President Gillette could feel the enthusiasm and spirit of missionary work in Amram. The scope of the mission President Gillette was responsible for overseeing was international, with many visitors from all over the world coming to see Temple Square, but this was an opportunity to reach outside the temple grounds. This could bless some lives in Africa. President Gillette immediately knew which sister missionaries he would assign. He smiled at the earnest request and the resolute determination of the man sitting in his office. President Gillette leaned forward in his chair and looked directly at Amram.

"When can we start?"

. . .

Amram locked eyes with the sister missionaries sitting across the small wooden table from him. Their eyebrows were all raised in anticipation as they heard the first ring. Then the second.

"Hello! Elder Musungu!" Dr. Weston answered. He could see from the phone number that it was the expected call from the Temple Square Visitors Center.

"*Muli bwanji*, Dr. Weston" Amram said. It was a customary greeting in the native Malawi dialect of Chichewa. Amram was familiar with a little of the language, but he would teach the missionary lessons in English.

"It's great to talk with you again," Amram continued. The first missionary lesson had been so encouraging, but it was always a relief when the investigator showed up for the second discussion. Amram smiled at the missionaries across the table.

"I am excited to learn more about your religion," Dr. Weston stated, "and actually I have invited some family and friends to hear you teach. We have about ten people here today. I hope that's okay?"

"Oh, wow, that is great," Amram replied. "Please continue to invite whoever would like to hear this great message of love and hope. All are welcome!"

After one month, the number of investigators grew to thirty people. They all gathered around Dr. Weston's cell phone on speaker to hear Amram and the missionaries explain the principles and inspiring messages of the gospel of Jesus Christ. Amram taught the gathering of investigators but also left time for the answering of questions. With such a large group of thirty, Amram wanted to be sure that all individual inquiries were addressed.

Each Saturday, Amram attended the earliest temple session then traveled to the Temple Square Visitors Center to sit with the missionaries, make the phone call to Dr. Weston, and teach all who met at Dr. Weston's home for the scheduled appointment. All discussions began with an opening prayer, usually offered by Dr. Weston, and concluded with a closing prayer. Teaching often continued beyond the appointed time, so Dr. Weston often called Amram on his cell phone at home. Slowly the number of investigators grew as word spread throughout the community in Kasungu. The people in Malawi were ready and excited to hear the good news of the gospel, and Amram could feel the enthusiasm as he communicated with the group.

In addition to confirming the progress of the lessons to President Gillette, Amram continued to update his friend Larry Barkdull on the astonishing growth in Malawi. It had all started with that first message on the social media page. Larry knew he had been inspired to pull Amram into the conversation. After the first email with Dr. Weston, Amram was off and running with his usual fervor for missionary work.

Weeks turned into months, and the leaves on the trees announced the passing of new seasons. It had been one year since Amram's first conversation with Dr. Weston. Amram dialed Larry's cell phone number to give him the newest update.

"Hi, Larry. I have great news," Amram announced. "Dr. Weston's group in Malawi has grown to more than a hundred people!"

There was a moment of silence as Larry swallowed the lump in his throat. This kind of growth was incredible. Larry's mind swirled with questions.

Who could have known Dr. Weston would possess such a passion for the gospel? Who could have known of his desire to bring others along with him? Who could have known that Amram would commit week after week teaching through a cell phone to investigators in Africa?

The answer to those questions was clear, and Larry felt it as a powerful testimony. *The Lord knew.*

"Amram, I don't know what to say . . ." Larry responded, ". . . that's just amazing. There's bound to be a branch of the Church over there soon. The people are clearly ready."

"Oh, they're ready, Larry," Amram replied. "In fact, I've been mailing some general conference talks from the prophets and Apostles to help with their learning, and they're all studying and reviewing the scriptural assignments I give to them. We've moved forward from the basics."

"The leadership of the Church who are overseeing areas in Africa need to know this information," Larry stated. "They'd be interested in the activity in Malawi."

"I agree, Larry," Amram replied. "I have a meeting set up with Elder L. Whitney Clayton tomorrow because he helps Elder David A. Bednar supervise the Church in Africa. I'll let you know what he says."

"Amram, you're doing a great work, my friend," Larry said. His eyes filled with tears as he considered the collection of eager investigators coming together with no meetinghouses and no formal guidelines or materials. They gathered in response to their own hearts testifying of new truths never heard before.

And they gathered to hear the voice of Amram.

· · ·

"Brother Musungu, we appreciate everything you have done for the people in Malawi. Your documentation of the timeline, the instruction you have provided, and the growth of investigators you have described is thorough and very helpful for our future decisions."

Amram was sitting across from the two members of the Quorum of the Seventy who were responsible for the research in Africa relative to the growth of the Church. He had diligently prepared for this meeting and hoped a decision could be made immediately that he could report back to Dr. Weston and the group.

"With no Church group officially set up in the area and no missionaries assigned to Malawi, we are not yet to the point of baptizing the people there. We are grateful for the update and your insight toward the future of the Church in that area, but we need to be organized in our approach. Please continue teaching them, Brother Musungu."

Amram felt his heart sink. It felt like a dead end, but Amram had faced situations that appeared to be impossible many times before. Once again, he would need to be patient, trust the Lord's timing, and then inspire Dr. Weston and his community to continue meeting together.

· · ·

The weather forecast in Kasungu, Malawi, was for a warm, sunny day with temperatures in the mid-eighties. It was October 2017, making it five years since that first missionary discussion. Dr. Weston stood back and admired the hard work he and others had put into their makeshift tent for church services. A wood frame was covered with a piece of plastic to protect from both rain and the hot sun.

The growth of the investigators in Dr. Weston's community had now grown to more than three hundred people. What had started inside his home had expanded beyond the walls of his home, and this tent would allow a better environment for the masses who came every Sunday to hear Elder Musungu teach over the phone.

Dr. Weston was excited to take a picture on Sunday to send to Elder Musungu so he could witness the new tent filled with family, friends, and others who hungered to learn more about Jesus Christ.

Dr. Weston loved to serve the people in his community. His heart swelled with joy in the humble beginnings of his home when more and more people came each Sunday to study with the group. Investigators traveled both short and long distances to attend, and Dr. Weston was happy to provide food and drink to all who came to participate. He strongly believed that every person had goodness in his or her soul, and he felt a real purpose in reaching out and motivating others to live together in peace. Constructing the new tent on his property as a church meetinghouse would further facilitate that mission as a peacemaker.

The mayor of Kasungu attended along with people in the community from every line of business and economic stature. Dr. Weston was well respected as a kind leader and one who genuinely cared for everyone. He was generous and humble as he continuously reached out to others.

Elder Musungu sent a few Church manuals and hymnbooks for the Malawi congregation as added resources for the people. Dr. Weston called Elder Musungu daily to answer both doctrinal and administrative questions as the Malawi group worked hard to assemble and organize themselves into three hours of worship that included a chapel service, a Sunday School class, and other classes for men, women, and children to gather and learn the doctrine.

Dr. Weston took one final look at the completed tent, then lifted his eyes to the heavens before turning back toward his home. He already knew the hymn he would suggest they all sing that first Sunday service in the tent.

"Thank you, God, for this miracle of growth. We will continue to worship as we gather in this tent each Sunday. And, dear God, we desire more than anything to be baptized. Bless us to be patient as we wait for that great opportunity. . . ."

Dr. Weston quietly hummed the first line of the hymn he had chosen as he slowly walked back through the long grass to his home across the property. Dr. Weston's heart burned as he considered all that he had been blessed with in his life. Now he would use those blessings to lift others. His deep, soulful voice moved from a beautiful melody to tender words as he raised his hand to his heart and began to sing.

Dearest children, God is near you,
Watching o'er you day and night,
And delights to own and bless you,
If you strive to do what's right.
He will bless you, He will bless you,
If you put your trust in him.

Dr. Weston teaching an investigator class in his backyard.

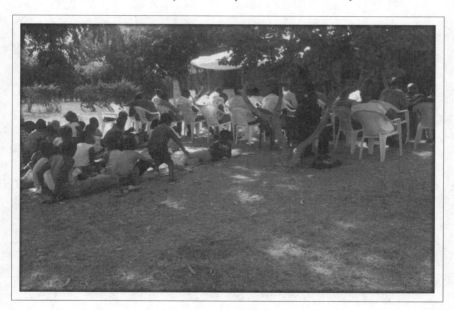

The number of investigators grows, and they are soon spilling outside of Dr. Weston's house.

The tent which is made from sacks, sits on Dr. Weston's property and is used to accommodate more than two hundred people.

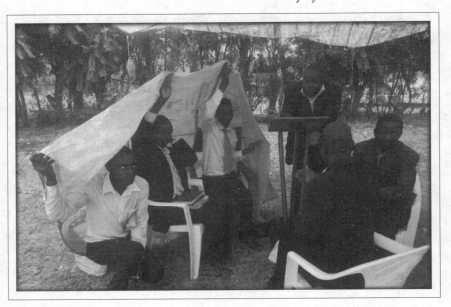

"Whilst in investigation meeting under the tent, heavy rain came with strong wind, but He protected us in His wings." —Dr. Weston

CHAPTER SEVENTEEN

We exercise appropriate faith in our Master
by involving ourselves in the work of the Master.

Robert Millet

"It's really amazing, Brother Musungu. The Malawi group is operating like a normal branch!" Elder Terence M. Vinson exclaimed.

"Yes, for quite some time," Amram confirmed.

Elder Vinson had listened intently to Amram's plea earlier that year regarding Dr. Weston Kapasule and the investigators gathering on his property. As a new member of the Presidency of the Seventy, he was now responsible for the Church in Africa, and Amram had brought the Malawi situation to his attention.

"After the October 2018 general conference, we contacted the Zambia Lusaka Mission President and the Area Authority Seventy from South Africa Area and had them visit Dr. Weston and attend the Sunday services there on his property," Elder Vinson explained. "They were astounded by the organization of it all."

"I have been teaching and working with Dr. Weston and others over there for six long years," Amram shared, "and they have gained an understanding of how to operate from Church manuals I sent over along with my assistance in answering questions over many phone calls."

"We have learned that this Malawi group is larger than all the branches combined in the entire Zambia mission!" Elder Vinson continued. "Brother Musungu, this is just incredible."

"Yes, Elder Vinson. The field is white in Kasungu and ready to harvest," Amram said with a smile. "These good people have patiently and prayerfully been waiting for baptism. Many of them have waited a very long time."

Elder Vinson considered the steadfast faith of the people in Malawi. It was almost beyond belief that they had not given up hope. They trusted that the blessings of baptism would eventually come to them in God's own timing. What an inspiring group of people.

"Brother Musungu, we are going to prepare for another visit," Elder Vinson said.

"Another visit?" Amram asked.

"Yes, another visit," Elder Vinson replied. "This group needs to be baptized."

Amram dropped his head into his hands and closed his eyes tightly. The words were staggering, and his heart began to pound in his chest as his mind tried to grasp the reality. He wanted to weep and shout for joy and fall to his knees all at the same time.

Oh, dear God my prayers have been answered. So many prayers. . . .

"Of course, Brother Musungu, we want you to fly over to meet these future Malawi Saints in person and perform some of the first baptisms."

Amram managed to find his voice. "Absolutely! Oh, yes, it would be such a great honor," Amram answered.

Tears began rolling down Amram's cheeks. His emotions were beginning to catch up to the unexpected announcement. He couldn't wait to call Dr. Weston.

"Thank you . . ." Amram humbly said. His voice was barely audible as it trailed off into deep, heartwarming thoughts.

It was a sentiment of gratitude to both Elder Vinson and to God.

"Thank you," he whispered.

.   .   .

Amram buckled his seatbelt in preparation for the first leg of the flight to Malawi. He would be in the air for more than fourteen hours, but Amram couldn't be happier to begin the journey. Some generous Salt Lake City friends in the Church had sponsored the purchase price of the international flight to Nairobi, Kenya, with a final leg arriving at Lilongwe, Malawi. Amram pulled the boarding pass out of his shirt pocket and read the date of January 27, 2020, in the left corner as a tender reminder that the day he had prepared, prayed, and fasted for over eight long years had finally arrived. He held the paper to his heart then slipped it back into his pocket. This was real!

As he pondered the reality of the moment, his thoughts suddenly switched from elation to sorrow. Larry had passed away from a heart attack two years earlier and would not see the miracles of their humble beginnings with Dr. Weston asking to know more. Amram closed his eyes and hoped that Larry was able to see this moment and feel the same emotions of fruition. Surely there was a celebration in heaven today as Larry witnessed the full circle.

As the plane lifted into the sky, Amram's thoughts flashed through hundreds of internal conversations he had with himself over the years.

Keep waiting. Don't give up. The Lord will do His work in His own time. Keep teaching and teaching. . . .

Conversations with hundreds of people in Malawi who had soft hearts and a strong desire to be baptized swirled in his mind.

Just wait. Be patient. They will come, and you will be happy. You will soon see all the blessings of the gospel in baptism.

These good people could easily have become discouraged by what appeared to be a lack of attention and concern from Church leadership. With no official meetinghouse or immediate response to requests to be baptized, they could have felt forgotten or unimportant. They could have given up. Instead, this community clung to a blind faith and Amram's persistent words that all would eventually be made right. That Church leadership *would* come. It was the most inspiring definition of faith Amram had ever seen.

Amram heard a quiet melody and whispered lyrics to a favorite hymn that would forever remind him of the Malawi people's faith.

He had thought of them often when he sang the song in Church meetings. Tear-filled eyes pondered their situation as he voiced the hopeful words:

> God moves in a mysterious way
> His wonders to perform;
> He plants his footsteps in the sea
> And rides upon the storm.
>
> Ye fearful Saints, fresh courage take;
> The clouds ye so much dread
> Are big with mercy and shall break
> In blessings on your head.
>
> His purposes will ripen fast,
> Unfolding ev'ry hour;
> The bud may have a bitter taste,
> But sweet will be the flower.

Amram leaned his head back on the headrest. In the three short days in Malawi, there would be so much to handle. He needed the Lord's hand and guidance from the Spirit to direct him in speaking words from his heart to the community. There would also be priesthood ordinations and administrative duties. And, of course, he wanted to spend some time with the youth. They were the next generation of promise in Malawi.

Amram reached under the airline seat in front of him and pulled out the scriptures in his bag. The first time he was on an international flight had been December of 1997; at that time, he had fifty dollars in his pocket and a testimony of hope in his heart. He needed the Lord's words now every bit as much as he had on that first flight to the United States.

Amram opened the worn cover of his scriptures, turned a few pages, and allowed his eyes to search the words with a prayer in his heart.

Lord, carry me to Malawi.

KENYA

Figure 10
Rural village girls.

CHAPTER EIGHTEEN

You have one business on earth—

to save souls.

John Wesley

"Elder Musungu is coming! He's coming to baptize us! God has answered our prayers!"

Those words were repeated over and over as news spread throughout the Malawi community. Full-time missionaries were quickly transferred into the area to begin baptismal interviews prior to Amram's arrival. Plans were made for the special baptismal day of February 1, 2020, and families everywhere wanted to be involved in the preparations and festivities.

One important detail was missing that would require hard work from everyone in the community: there was no baptismal font. But the faithful group found a solution and came together to create their own.

There was a quiet, secluded place where the cows came to drink. A small pond lined with cement functioned as a watering hole for the animals. The night before Amram was to arrive, all families came with buckets and scrub brushes to transform the watering hole into a font.

Men, women, and children used buckets to drain the filthy water out of the hole, then dropped to their knees with brushes and rags and scrubbed the cement walls until they were clean. The people took pride in their project as they considered the holy ordinance that would be performed the following day. This was *their* special baptismal font where the very first baptisms in Malawi would take place.

After the cement hole was thoroughly cleaned, they connected a pipe that slowly filled it with water. Families grabbed their buckets and used water from secondary sources to add water as quickly as possible. They worked tirelessly throughout the night so it would be ready. A newly constructed baptismal font plus one white baptismal jumpsuit was preparation enough to perform the baptisms. They felt a sense of pride and elation for the momentous occasion. With multiple baptisms happening the following day, the jumpsuit would have to be shared by all.

The community finally stood back to admire their efforts as the sun began to rise over the grassy plain. The font wasn't perfectly clean, but it was good enough. The water temperature was cold, but the anticipation of the sacred event warmed their hearts and buoyed their spirits. They were witnessing a miracle and felt grateful to have used their hands to prepare the holy space.

. . .

Amram ran through the streets of Nairobi racing against the clock. He had only two days to do some missionary work in the city before his final evening flight to Malawi. The memories of serving his full-time mission in Kenya consumed his soul as he hurried through crowded neighborhoods and city streets wearing a backpack filled with copies of the Book of Mormon. The same missionary fervor that propelled his feet forward to do the Lord's work more than twenty years earlier still filled his soul. How he loved the people in Africa!

Amram shared his testimony with several Kenyans in the street, but his ultimate destination was government offices. He had the opportunity to share a Book of Mormon with Musalia Mudavadi, the former vice-president of Kenya and current deputy prime minister. In addition, he was able to meet with former Prime Minister Raila Odinga. Amram testified and shared the Book of Mormon with several government ministers in Nairobi with a prayer in his heart that they might feel the Spirit and have a desire to learn more. Amram knew that a righteous leadership could make a real difference in the lives of his fellow Kenyans.

Amram's mother and a few siblings were able to travel from their village for a short visit with him in Nairobi while he was there. It was the first time Amram had been able to see his family since his father died. It was a sweet reunion of catching up and remembering heartwarming memories from earlier days. Amram told his mother about the inspirational people in Malawi and the upcoming baptisms. He hoped the Church would one day find its way to his village so his entire family could have the chance to embrace the gospel. Pictures of Amram and his mother were taken to capture a moment's glimpse of a brief visit and an enduring love between the two.

Amram's last stop was a small Church distribution center in Nairobi, where he purchased some scriptures and other Church materials for the future Saints in Malawi. He loaded as much as would fit into his backpack and clutched the bag of remaining supplies under his arm as he raced toward the airport. The sun was sinking in the horizon, and his plane would be leaving soon.

With critical stops in Kenya complete, it was time to board the evening flight for Lilongwe, Malawi. Amram knew Dr. Weston would be at the airport along with the Lilongwe mayor and two other eager investigators to greet and drive him to Kasungu. Amram was physically tired from the ambitious schedule in Kenya, but he felt energized by the thought of finally meeting all the amazing Malawians in person. The true purpose for the trip and highlight of his life was just hours away.

. . .

Amram stood wearing a white shirt and tie as a symbol of his life's work as a missionary and walked over to stand next to Dr. Weston in the front of the tent the congregation had been meeting in. Together they faced the sea of eager investigators dressed in their colorful attire to celebrate the occasion. Amram's eyes welled up with tears, and he felt a wall of emotion in his chest. What beautiful people! The moment was almost surreal as his eyes finally met those he had taught, counseled, and helped to understand the teachings of Jesus Christ.

"This is the man who was talking to you on the phone for the past eight years," Dr. Weston announced.

Tears fell down the cheeks of the Malawians as they saw the man behind the voice that had testified and taught them for so many years. Some clapped their hands in joy while others wept.

"He has come all the way from the United States to baptize us today. We honor him and thank God for this answer to so many prayers."

Amram smiled at the sight before him and cleared his throat, hoping the lump in his throat would allow him to speak the words in his heart.

"Hello, my dear brothers and sisters," Amram said with a loud voice that could be heard throughout the crowd.

Eyes widened at the recognized sound. To hear in person the voice of the man who taught them the gospel brought another round of cheers and tears. Testimonies were strengthened and faith was sustained as their revered missionary shared his feelings of love for them and for the Savior. Hearts beat in unison as affirmations and emotions unified the group as one. In this sacred moment, every individual embraced something felt within that humble tent—the Savior's love and the love of the missionary who had helped them find it.

The crowd gathered around their baptismal font and watched as Amram and Dr. Weston waded into the cold water. It seemed appropriate that Dr. Weston be the first of this group to be baptized. Amram raised his right hand and pronounced the baptismal ordinance before lowering Dr. Weston into the water. Those in attendance held their breath to witness such a long-awaited event. When Dr. Weston was lifted and arose from the water, he immediately wrapped his arms around his missionary's neck. They stood together in an embrace, recognizing the historic moment as the crowd looked on.

As each new member emerged from the font, the soaking, cold jumpsuit was removed in a small enclosure near the font and handed to the next individual for baptism. City Mayor Jere was the second baptism, and so it continued throughout the day until fifty-six people were baptized that day by Amram.

Following the baptisms, Dr. Weston had food and drinks for everyone in a beautiful celebration of the day's events. It allowed Amram the opportunity to personally greet many members of the community who attended. Amram felt the great spirit of the people there and treasured tender moments with the Malawi saints.

Amram thought of his own nephew, who was currently serving a mission in the Zambia Lusaka Mission. His nephew was the son of Benson, the cousin who Amram had introduced to the missionaries in Kenya. Amram was amazed at how things had come full circle and that family members were now harvesting the same field that Amram had planted nine years earlier. It humbled Amram to consider the scope of the Lord's hand in both his individual life and the lives of those in his beloved family.

Later that evening, Amram shook hands with the full-time missionaries who had been transferred to the area to assist with the baptismal interviews and events of the weekend. They appeared weary from a very long weekend. Amram was happy to see the fatigue on their faces.

"You'd better be okay getting wet, because you're going to spend a lot of time baptizing these people," Amram said with a smile. "This is only the beginning."

. . .

The next day brought warm sunshine and soft, cool breezes that seemed to usher in the Sabbath day and another opportunity to gather under the church tent. The newly baptized members along with friends and family were eager to hear from their cherished missionary once more before he returned to the United States.

"Blessings will come into your lives," Amram said. "You will see them in your own lives and the lives of your family and friends if you live faithful to your baptismal covenant."

After Amram concluded his address as part of the church services, he presided over a stream of priesthood ordinations as Dr. Weston and others were ordained to the office of priest. That gave them the authority to assist the missionaries in future baptisms of family members and friends in Kasungu and to begin administering the sacrament for their church services. Dr. Weston immediately acted with that authority and baptized both his wife and son on that very Sunday.

It had been a very long and emotional weekend for Amram, but there was still one important group he wanted to address: the youth. Amram understood that strong young men and women would build a good generation to come.

Amram stood before forty teenagers and bore testimony of rising from difficult challenges and clinging to faith and hope. He talked of his own conversion and challenged them to serve their own missions. Amram had the full attention of the youth as he affirmed the miracles in his life and his own desire to pay those blessings forward.

"It is important that you elevate yourselves to a higher level of living. You are disciples of Christ. Cling to the light that is within each of you and find your purpose," Amram professed.

He paused to make direct eye contact with each young person.

"Promise me you will stay out of trouble. You are better than that because you are here on earth to do great things."

Heads nodded in agreement. Young hearts burned as they pondered their own worth.

"I've brought something for you," Amram said with a smile. He knew this would be a healthy distraction from roaming the streets, where kids so often found trouble. He leaned over and unzipped a large, canvas bag. All attention was on Amram.

"Soccer balls and team jerseys!" Amram declared as he held a few up in the air.

"Wow!" the young people cheered. "I want to play!" several shouted.

"I'll talk with some of the parents and see if we can get a team organized with a coach. It's going to require practice and discipline," Amram announced. "Can you commit to that?"

As many heads in the audience nodded, an older boy said, "Thank you." His eyes glistened, and he came forward to extend a hand. Amram shook the older boy's hand and was surprised by the firm grip. Their eyes locked for a moment as the two felt a mutual understanding of love and trust. Amram had prayed that he might make a small difference in the lives of the rising generation here in Malawi. Perhaps he had.

"You're welcome, Son," Amram whispered.

. . .

"One year later and the growth is still continuing at a rapid pace," Dr. Weston said. "I wish you were here to see it. Missionary work is exploding, and we have more than two hundred members! That's the largest attendance in the entire Zambia Lusaka Mission!"

"Oh, that is music to my soul," Amram replied. "I'm still speaking with the branch presidency and elders quorum president a couple of times each month. They are working very hard."

Amram knew from talking to the Zambia Lusaka Mission president that the mission boundaries had been extended to include Malawi. A large, diverse group of missionaries from the United States, Democratic Republic of Congo, Nigeria, Kenya, and other African countries were now serving in Malawi. Because of the explosion in investigators and baptisms, there were more missionaries now assigned to the Malawi area than to the entire rest of the Zambia Lusaka Mission. Church members believed that sharing the gospel would fortify their city and bring joy to all the surrounding communities, and their resulting eager discussions with friends and family were creating a wave of interest.

Amram hoped a second new Malawi mission would be formed soon. The Malawi mission would be primarily an English-speaking mission, but another main language spoken there was Chichewa. The Book of Mormon was currently in the process of being translated to Chichewa. How that would benefit the missionary work there!

"Well, Dr. Weston, it has been just more than a year since that beautiful day of baptisms," Amram added, "so it's time to begin preparing for a visit to the Johannesburg South Africa Temple."

"Oh, yes, we've talked about that," Dr. Weston reported, "and I want to take my family to be sealed there very soon. In fact, I have more great news."

"More great news?" Amram questioned. "It's *all* great news! What else is happening?"

"My wife and I are expecting twins," Dr. Weston said with excitement.

"Twins?" Amram exclaimed. "Is this your way of doubling up on the growth of the Lord's kingdom over there?"

The two men laughed at the comical comparison.

"You know, Dr. Weston, when I was there last year, I could envision a new temple in Malawi," Amram stated. "I saw sites over there and thought to myself, *Wow, that would be a great place for a temple.* Your land is rich in resources, and the fertility of the land produces most of the food for the country and other neighboring cities. I believe the Church will build a temple there very soon."

The two men pondered the possibility. Once strangers living across the world from each other, the two hearts now fully united in friendship with a common desire to share the joy of the gospel with the world.

"In the Lord's timing," Amram continued. "In the Lord's timing. . . ."

"Let us pray for it together," Dr. Weston replied.

Amram baptizing Dr. Weston

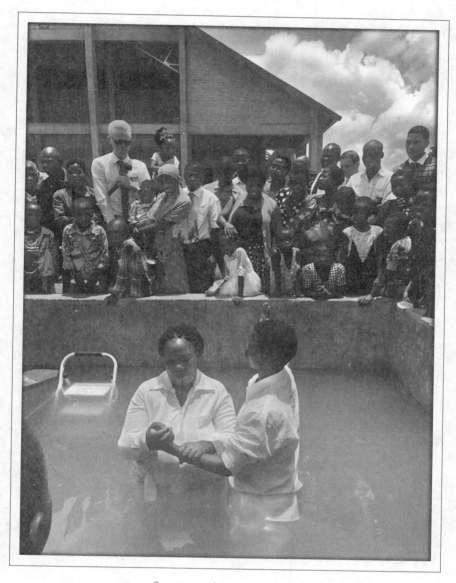

Dr. Weston baptizing his wife

Group of young men and women that Amram spoke to on Sunday.

CHAPTER NINETEEN

The work of the Lord is done by ordinary people

who work in an extraordinary way.

Gordon B. Hinckley

"What? You're running for President of Kenya? Amram, why?" Freddie Thomas asked. "Why would you run for President? And why . . . why would you go back to Kenya?"

Amram laughed at the shocked sound of surprise in the cracked, high-pitched voice on the other end of the line as Freddie tried to absorb the unthinkable news. It was a friendship born from missionary work when Elder Freddie Thomas taught the gospel to Amram as a teenager, a friendship that was then strengthened as the two spent months together as companions in the mission field. Amram had kept in touch with Freddie over the years as they both matured and ventured forward in their own lives, raising children and building careers in the United States.

"Freddie, I can help the people. I know I can make a difference."

"I would never stand in your way, Amram. Of course, you can make a difference. You're always thinking about the people,"

Freddie said. "My family will always support you, and if you win . . . well, I'm going to go to Kenya to cheer for you," Freddie promised.

Freddie shouldn't have been surprised. No one had greater faith and ambition than Amram, and his focus was always on making life better for the poor and the needy. Few exhibited such drive and dedication.

Amram was simply unstoppable.

. . .

The 2017 Presidential race in Kenya was a tight one. Seven candidates with decades of corruption and government control were attempting to persuade most of the Kenyan voters, but some members of parliament knew of Amram and his popularity with people throughout the country as well as his relationship with several leaders in high government positions. A few members of parliament knew the country needed honest, trustworthy leadership, and they felt Amram was the answer.

When the invitation to run was pitched to Amram, his mind wandered back twenty years to his campaign for student body president at Ensign College. He had gathered up some ambitious students to support him on a campaign team and picked the marketing slogan of *Your Brother, Your Leader.* In Amram's campaign speech, he told the student audience that he was committed to making lives better at the college, but that one day he would be a political leader in Kenya or the United States. From that day forward, everyone called him "President." Even now, the nickname had stuck with him for two decades. Amram chuckled at the thought that perhaps he had become comfortable with the nickname for a reason.

Amram had closely followed political campaigns in Kenya for years and was troubled by the corruption and political unrest happening in the east African nation. He worried about Kenya's national security problems, high unemployment rate, and economic troubles. So often politicians campaigned on the platform of *change,* but despite their promises and rhetoric, corruption often took hold once they held office. Only families and friends of the rich had opportunities. It broke Amram's heart as he longed to see everyone treated fairly.

"I want to help the women, children, and the forgotten people with disabilities in Kenya who are struggling," Amram said.

His wife, Noelle, nodded. She knew his soft heart and understood the respect and devotion Amram held for his own mother, who had done her best raising her own children in poor and humble circumstances with no apparent opportunities.

"All children in Kenya should be attending school," Amram continued. "The resources are there, and we just need to organize scholarships and additional funding for schools. Education will open doors for their future; I've seen that in my own life. An educated upcoming generation will support a strong economy for Kenya."

"I know you, Amram," Noelle responded. "Nobody works

harder than you, and if you are feeling pulled down this path, then we'll do it together."

Amram smiled at his beautiful, supportive wife. What a bright light she was in his life.

"Nothing is impossible as long as it has to do with blessing the lives of others, right?" Amram said as their eyes met. "I just want to spread peace and prosperity to help the good people of Kenya thrive. I feel such a deep love for them. . . ."

Amram's voice trailed off as the two stood hand in hand, pondering what their future might look like. The Presidential nomination was going to be a longshot, but Amram's wife and children stood solidly behind his decision to enter the race. If Amram won, the family would move to Kenya. Perhaps Kenya was ready for real change! If it was the Lord's will, Amram was up for the challenge to lead that change.

.   .   .

"Our campaign is going to be very peaceful," Amram told his team. "We will definitely stick to the message. No pointing fingers. No insulting anybody. I believe the Kenyans are tired of negative politics."

Amram had a small campaign team in Salt Lake City willing to support his desire to enter the race in Kenya. His campaign manager, Swen Howard, had served a mission in Kenya at the same time as Amram, so his love for the Kenyans and experience working with Amram motivated him to jump into the ring.

Initially, the team created a platform on social media to spread the message to the 52 million people living in Kenya. Amram addressed his humble beginnings and promised to represent *every* person in Kenya, regardless of their wealth. He hoped to visit all the people in the villages and listen to their pleas. Through his media campaign, he assured the people that millions of disadvantaged groups of men, women, and children stood to benefit most from his ideas.

Amram spoke of his desire that each of the forty-eight tribes in Kenya be represented so they could create laws to benefit everyone. With all tribes having a voice, perhaps they could work together for the good of the country. That would attract investors, who would then trust the stability of the Kenyan people and its economy. Kenya's position on the continent of Africa was the center of strength for technology and other international organizations, such as the United Nations, World Health Organization, and others headquartered there. More activity and trust from international businesses would certainly create jobs for the people.

When it came time to choose a running mate, Amram promised to select a woman, because women were underrepresented. He believed women play an important role in uniting a country and wanted their voices to be heard. As President of Kenya, he vowed his cabinet would eventually be comprised of 50 percent men and 50 percent women.

Amram's vast network of political support in both the state of Utah and the United States government encouraged him in his quest to run. In addition, he had support from many in the international business community who believed Amram's moral core and philosophy for a better life in Kenya gave him strength as a future leader. All who met Amram knew he possessed endless optimism and enthusiasm for life and the ability to draw out the very best of those around him.

. . .

"I will be the best President this country has ever had," Amram declared.

It was a short visit to Kenya with his campaign manager to secure the paperwork and funding required to run for the office of President. In his travels, Amram never missed an opportunity to speak to a crowd of people. His name was already circulating in the Kenya media and publications, and he was gaining more and more attention.

His message from one group to another was consistent: "I have risen out of poverty myself, and with better laws and honest government I will help you gain control of your country."

A political party in Kenya had accepted Amram and nominated him to run. Amram would be the youngest man running for the office. He was in Nairobi at a bank to secure campaign accounts at the financial institution. As Amram and Swen waited in the bank lobby for the completion of a wire transfer, a man in a suit approached the two men. The man extended his hand in a friendly greeting then looked directly at Amram.

"You've been noticed, and people are talking about you," the man said. "I know someone who is very interested in your campaign and would like to meet with you."

The three men shook hands and agreed to meet at a designated office in downtown Nairobi later that day. Amram was both curious and cautiously optimistic about the meeting. Political ventures in Kenya were often messy and dangerous.

.   .   .

Amram and Swen arrived at the meeting to learn it was a meeting with an opponent running in the race for President. The opponent's team was respectful but very direct.

"Your name has come up at the National Intelligence of Kenya office," the man said. "We have a contact there at the Intelligence office who has confirmed they are talking about you."

Amram understood this meant trouble. Violence was a common element in elections there, and Amram knew killings were ordered for people who stood in the way of those who saw things differently. Amram was surprised how quickly his name and reputation among the people had gained popularity. Clearly, it had raised some flags.

"Mr. Musungu, our candidate is older in age. If you throw your support behind him this year, we will endorse you in the next election. It would be a wise decision to consider this offer."

Weeks later, Amram and his campaign staff sat around a large table in Salt Lake City to consider all the facts they had along with their meager financial resources. After the return trip to Kenya to file the paperwork, they sat together to discuss the situation and make some important decisions. There had already been quiet talk of a private ceremony to swear in a new Kenyan president by force. Such talk had escalated the distrust of government, and violence was on the rise as a result.

After everyone's input, Amram stood at the head of the table to speak.

"Given the messy circumstances in the Kenyan elections and the absence of a full security team to protect me and my family over there, I believe we should postpone my run for President of Kenya," Amram announced. "The timing doesn't feel right, and I think we should step aside for now."

Amram was discouraged with the change of plans, but the 2017 bid didn't feel right.

"We have learned a lot, and people in parliament and other political offices are still calling me from Kenya for new ideas and possibilities," Amram continued. "Perhaps this was a journey to grasp and review strategies for a future run."

Amram looked at his staff with adoration and respect for the time they had given in support.

"The Lord will let me know what future door he wants me to open," Amram concluded.

Amram's team was in full support of his difficult decision. Amram's hope had been contagious, and those around him in both Kenya and the United States believed he might be able to make a difference in politics. It felt as though Amram's life had prepared him for leadership, and there was no doubt he possessed the qualities and energy to influence the political scope in Kenya. But they agreed with Amram: the timing wasn't right.

"I want to be the Lord's instrument," Amram concluded. "I love to serve the people and I know their cries. My heart is with the women and the children in Kenya, and I want to help them. If the Lord wants me to be there on the gospel side, I will do it. If He wants me there on the political side, I will do it. With the help of the Lord, nothing is impossible."

The scene around the table was thick with emotion. The team respected and admired this future leader standing before them. Several were nodding their heads in agreement with the spoken words from his heart.

"I know God can help me build bridges to bless many lives."

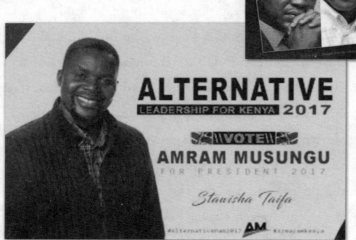

Current President of Kenya Uhuru Kenyatta, Amram, and the opposition leader in 2017.

Amram with U.S. Representative Mia Love at the Republican convention.

U.S. Representative Chris Stewart with Amram.

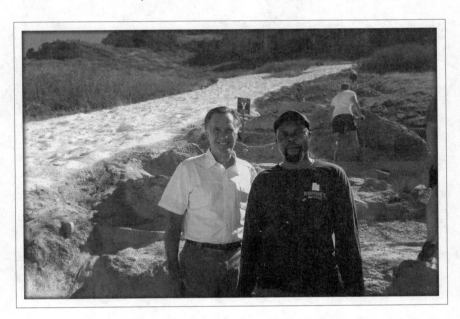

Amram hiking to the "Y" in Provo, Utah with Mitt Romney.

Amram on the baptism day of his two children.

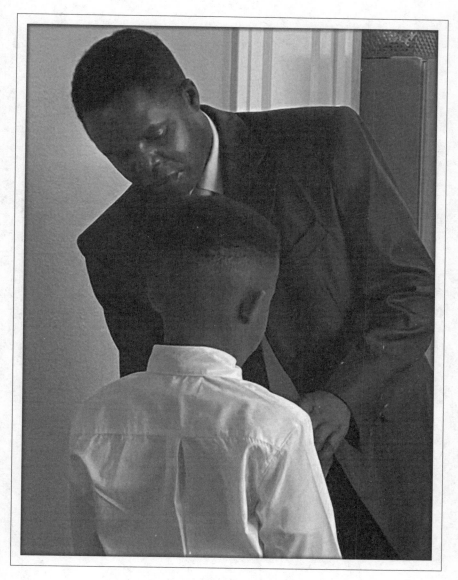

Amram today helping his son get ready for church.

KENYA

Figure 11

School teacher and her students.

AFTERWORD

"There is no impossible in life."

Amram Musungu

Amram must have said that a dozen times during months of interviews in my preparation to write his story. He believes it with his whole heart and soul, and after writing his story, I'm inclined to believe it too.

I've talked with hundreds of missionaries throughout my life, but no one quite like Amram. The fire in his soul is inspiring, meritorious, and contagious. The characteristics admired in Amram are not simply perceived when he promotes at pulpits or other engagements, but something he quietly and intentionally *lives*.

Perhaps one of the most noble callings in this life is that of teacher. We learn through people's words and actions then consider how we can adapt in our own life what we've gained. Amram's life teaches both a wealth of enlightenment and a stirring in our own soul to be a little better. Give a little more. Share our light and make a difference in the world.

Following are a few quotes from Amram that grabbed my heart.

"Life without prayer is like eating food without salt."

Amram learned the importance of prayers from both parents as he watched them pray over everything in their lives. If food was on the table, they offered thanks, and when the family had to go without, there were prayers of gratitude for other recognized blessings. In his family, the purpose of prayers became a means of communicating with God, and it was natural for Amram to continue an ongoing dialogue with God in his later teenage years. Amram might not have found his testimony and membership in The Church of Jesus Christ of Latter-day Saints if he had not been talking to God about his life and purpose.

As difficulties deepened and circumstances felt impossible, it was natural for Amram to turn to prayer. He has never claimed a blessing or miraculous event in his life was anything other than an answer to prayer. Amram is an example of pouring his questions and concerns into prayer, appreciating patience in God's timing, and opening his heart to recognize promptings and glimmers of hope in all their unique and varied forms.

Regardless of current events and conditions in his life, Amram always partners with God. The power comes from Amram's follow-through. He *acts* on those answers.

"Heavenly Father knows when and how to lift me up and how to fight for me. He's done that every single second of my life."

Amram's faith is unbreakable and knows no boundaries. He believes God is the author of everything and will ultimately show His hand in the details of his life. Often, we don't see His influence during the struggle, but Amram will testify that it often comes later through friends and family members. Amram trusts that God has and will always put him in the right place at the right time.

Amram recently asked his now-widowed mother if she ever felt afraid living alone. She explained to her son that she does not feel frightened because she knows that God loves her and is watching over her home. That kind of faith and conviction has seen her through many difficult circumstances. Amram learned at her feet as a young boy and is still listening and adopting that characteristic in his adult life.

Daily scripture stories told in his childhood home bolstered his faith then and now. Stories of the prophets testify that God will provide a way for His work to be done. Jonah received it in the form of a fish. Amram received it in the form of two missionaries who changed a barefoot boy's life and ultimately inspired him to find a way out of one of the largest slums in the world. Amram's message to all of us is to *never say never* when we have a mission to accomplish.

Amram continues to teach hundreds of people in Kenya. There is a large group of people in the city of Embu who live outside the mission boundaries. Once again, Amram has become *their* missionary by teaching over the cell phone as they wait for the Church to authorize baptisms and a new branch. Amram's faith bolsters his own belief that this will happen in the Lord's way, and his unwavering faith acts as the rope that the people in Embu hold tightly as they patiently wait. The gospel and his own life experiences have taught Amram that nothing is impossible if it has to do with blessing the lives of others.

"I rejoice every day, and I want to share what I have with people. My missionary nametag is on my heart, and it never comes off."

Amram attributes the joy in his life to the gospel. Every soul who he brings to Christ multiplies that gift. Every year when Amram sets personal goals in his life, missionary work is at the top of the list. Amram doesn't just meet his goals, he exceeds them. Whether it's volunteering to tag along with the full-time missionaries in Salt Lake City, singing with the Tabernacle Choir, testifying to people he meets in grocery stores or on the street, or teaching large groups of investigators in Africa via cell phone, Amram never misses the opportunities he prays to find. He says if he had to choose between eating and teaching, he would choose teaching. When I ask how many individuals he's brought into the membership of the Church, he says there are too many to count.

Amram's joy is visible and contagious because it's authentic. Because he lives what he believes, his life is evidence that missionary work is both simple and powerful. It begins with a smile to those placed in our path. A good starting point can be *hello* or *jambo*. Amram believes we can all put ourselves in his shoes and rise up to be missionaries to the world as we lift and bring hope to those who are searching.

What does the future hold for Amram? He is waiting for God to open a door. Whether that is here in the United States or in Africa remains to be seen. He will serve where he is needed with his family standing right beside him.

His advice to those in Africa and essentially to all of us is this: *Think big and rely on God.* That mindset is what brought a barefoot boy out of the slum to journey forward to the United States with only fifty dollars in his pocket, and it's the same thing that caused him to ultimately make a run for President of Kenya. Amram's life is testimony to one truth he wants to share with the world.

God will build a bridge.

KENYA

Figure 12
Kenyan landscape.

"May we never forget

the route we took to get here

And the Captain of the ship

that brought us."

Nellie Ashdown
Dec 20, 2003

In a handwritten letter to Amram
expressing great joy at seeing
him sing with the Tabernacle Choir.
She was in her nineties.

BIBLIOGRAPHY

Anon. "We Are Sowing." *Hymns of the Church of Jesus Christ of Latter-day Saints.* Salt Lake City: The Church of Jesus Christ of Latter-day Saints, 1985.

AskMayoExpert. "Extracorporeal membrane oxygenation (ECMO)." *Mayo Clinic*, 2019.

Bullock, William. "We Love Thy House, O God." *Hymns of the Church of Jesus Christ of   Latter-day Saints.* Salt Lake City: The Church of Jesus Christ of Latter-day Saints, 1985.

Cowper, William. "God Moves in a Mysterious Way." *Hymns of the Church of Jesus Christ of Latter-day Saints.* Salt Lake City: The Church of Jesus Christ of Latter-day Saints, 1985.

Creamer, Tami J. "I Know That My Savior Loves Me." *Additional Songs for Children.* Salt Lake City: The Church of Jesus Christ of Latter-day Saints, 2006-present.

Crowell, Grace Noll. "Because I Have Been Given Much." *Hymns of the Church of Jesus Christ of Latter-day Saints.* Salt Lake City: The Church of Jesus Christ of Latter-day Saints, 1985.

Curtis, Theodore E. "Come unto Him." *Hymns of the Church of Jesus Christ of Latter-day Saints.* Salt Lake City: The Church of Jesus Christ of Latter-day Saints, 1985.

Fowler, William. "We Thank Thee, O God, for a Prophet." *Hymns of the Church of Jesus Christ of Latter-day Saints.* Salt Lake City: The Church of Jesus Christ of Latter-day Saints, 1985.

Hart, John L. "Pioneer Day Races attract Field of 3,300." *Church News*, 1999.

Pollard, Josephine. "I Have Work Enough to Do." *Hymns of the Church of Jesus Christ of Latter-day Saints.* Salt Lake City: The Church of Jesus Christ of Latter-day Saints, 1985.

Snow, Eliza R., "O My Father." *Hymns of the Church of Jesus Christ of Latter-day Saints.* Salt Lake City: The Church of Jesus Christ of Latter-day Saints, 1985.

Walker, Charles L., "Dearest Children, God Is Near You." *Hymns of the Church of Jesus Christ of Latter-day Saints.* Salt Lake City: The Church of Jesus Christ of Latter-day Saints, 1985.

Watts, Isaac. "Sweet Is the Work." *Hymns of the Church of Jesus Christ of Latter-day Saints.* Salt Lake City: The Church of Jesus Christ of Latter-day Saints, 1985.

REFERENCES

Kenya Photography:

Figure 1: Kilimanjaro. By Jürgen Böhm - CC0 Public Domain Photo from pixabay.com

Figure 2: Elephants. By Edwin van Wijk - CC0 Public Domain Photo from pixabay.com

Figure 3: Dusty Landscape and Wildlife in Kenya (5/17). By Jordi Fernandez - CC0 Public Domain Photo from goodfreephotos.com

Figure 4: Nairobi, Kenya Street Crowded. By Nina Stock - CC0 Public Domain Photo from pixabay.com

Figure 5: Tribesman looking at the landscape of Kenya (11/17). By Sho Hatakeyama. - CC0 Public Domain Photo from goodfreephotos.com

Figure 6: African Women Walking Along Sand Road To Mapai. By Jean van der Meulen - CC0 Public Domain Photo from pixabay.com

Author and motivational speaker, Heidi Tucker.

ABOUT THE AUTHOR

Heidi Tucker has won multiple Book of the Year and Best Inspirational Book Awards for all three of her books, *The Secret Keepers, Finding Hope in the Journey* and *Servie's Song*. Her passion for writing and speaking about light and hope has inspired thousands. Heidi is known as a great storyteller who motivates others to rise up and find new strength. Through her writing and speaking, she teaches how to find hope in your own journey and make a difference.

When Heidi isn't writing her next book or speaking at a conference, you'll find her spending time outdoors with her husband, four grown children, and eleven grandchildren. She loves sunflowers, hiking, and ice cream . . . not necessarily in that order.

Find out more about Heidi, her books, and her social media platforms at HeidiTucker.com

ALSO BY HEIDI TUCKER

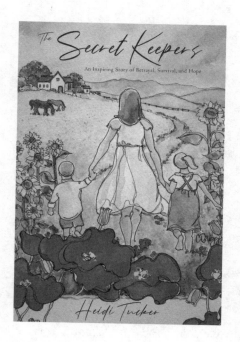

2021 Enduring Light Inspirational Award

The tragic and triumphant true story of Margi who rises up from horrific childhood abuse and trauma to uncover deep secrets. Her touching story will both enlighten and uplift as you witness her valiant conquest to reach for unshakable faith and hope. It is an unforgettable story that exemplifies love, courage, and triumph over seemingly insurmountable odds.

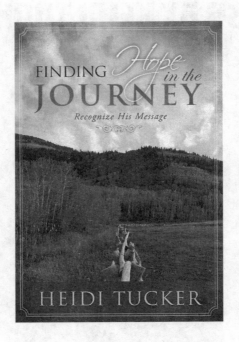

2019 BOOK OF THE YEAR FINALIST

There are glimpses of hope all around that are unique and divinely meant just for you. You will find them by watching, listening, and tuning all your senses. Heidi's inspiring words will help you learn to position your heart, mind, and soul to recognize quiet messages of hope from God.

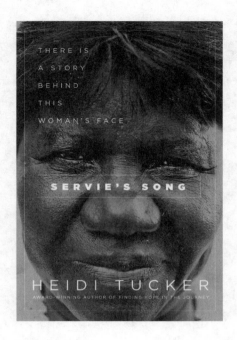

THERE IS
A STORY
BEHIND
THIS
WOMAN'S FACE

SERVIE'S SONG

HEIDI TUCKER

AWARD-WINNING AUTHOR OF FINDING HOPE IN THE JOURNEY

2018 BEST INSPIRATIONAL

One woman's emotional journey from tragedy and heartbreak to an inspiring path of hope and triumph. This true story of a woman's journey from Africa to the United States to rescue her children from poverty will motivate you to grab onto your faith and move forward trusting that you are never alone.